THUNDER RIVER

A TEXAS GAME WARDEN'S STORY

BENNY RICHARDS

THUNDER RIVER
A Texas Game Warden's Story

©2023 Benny Richards

ISBN: 979-8-218-15826-2 (Paperback)
ISBN: 979-8-218-15827-9 (ePub)

Book design and layout: Lighthouse24

The stories in this book are true, firsthand accounts of events that occurred during my career. The people and places are real. However, in order to protect them and their families from further persecution and embarrassment, the names of suspects and violators have been changed. No words or statements contained within this book are intended to cast doubt on or damage the reputation of any person or persons.

As author of this book, I represent no one other than myself. The thoughts and opinions contained inside are mine alone.

THUNDER RIVER

ABOUT THE AUTHOR

BENNY RICHARDS was born and raised in Hunt County, Texas. He spent his youth hunting, fishing, and picking up arrowheads in the fields and rivers in Northeast Texas. These experiences would serve him well as a Texas State Game Warden years later.

A graduate of East Texas State University in Commerce, Texas, Benny used his education to launch a career in law enforcement. He became a police officer in Richardson, Texas, in October, 1993. After a short but successful tour of duty there, he entered the Texas Game Warden Training Center in Austin, Texas, on January 1, 1996.

His first duty assignment after graduation was in Delta County. During his game warden career, Benny was stationed in numerous counties, mostly in Northeast, Texas, but he served all across Texas on different assignments. Benny received various awards and commendations throughout his career, including being named the Shikar Safari Wildlife Officer of the Year in 2015.

His love of storytelling led Benny to publish a weekly column called "Furry Tales" in his local newspaper and two other books. In addition to his reputation of being one of Texas' finest game wardens, Benny is probably best known for his role in the popular TV show Lone Star Law that aired on Animal Planet. Benny makes his home now near the small community of Campbell, Texas.

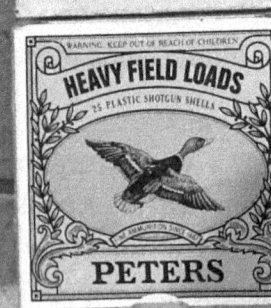

This book is dedicated to the memory of the 20 brave Texas Game Wardens who made the ultimate sacrifice and gave their lives in service to the citizens of the great state of Texas.

Joe Williams	James Daughtrey
Harry Raymond	James Birmingham
Dawson Murchison	Barry Decker
Richard Wynne, Jr.	Bruce Hill
Gus Engeling	Mike Pauling
Claude Keller	Wes Wagstaff
John David Murphree	Justin Hurst
Joseph Evans	Teyran Patterson
Lloyd Gustin	George Whatley, Jr.
Ronnie Germany	Christopher Wilson

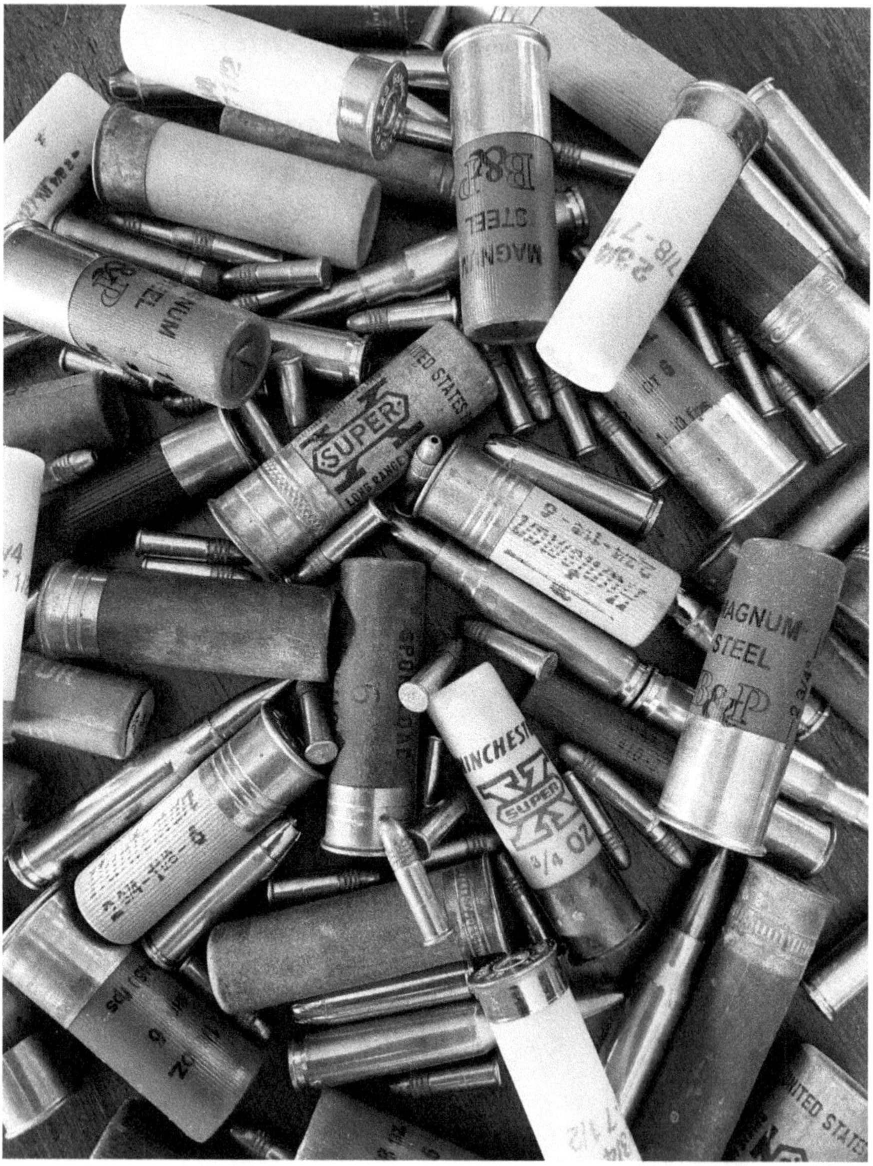
MAGNUM
STEEL
B&P
SUPER
LONG RANGE
SUPER
3/4 OZ

A game warden's job is to protect,
the woods and waters he must not neglect.

All the beasts large and small,
whether walking or crawling he must watch over them all.

The fish in the water and birds in the air,
they are all God's creatures placed under his care.

The task at hand is to preserve the land,
this will require a gun and a badge,
and a dependable man.

CONTENTS

FOREWORD

I KNEW SOMETHING WAS UP that night. Benny called me and said, "Hey, let's get dressed up nice and go downtown (Dallas) tonight." Of course I said ok. Most of our dates so far had consisted of wading through muddy creeks with walking sticks or cooking over campfires. My second clue that night would be different was the small, hard square box I had felt in the pocket of his sport's jacket when he slung it across the front seat of his truck and I happened to rest my hand on it. I thought, *Yep, this is it! Tonight's the night.*

We went to a nice restaurant in downtown Dallas and had a candlelit dinner and I was sure it would happen. Nope. Next up was a horse drawn carriage ride through the streets of downtown but still he didn't pop the question. Wrong again. I was beginning to wonder if I had imagined the little box in his jacket and the reason for the night out on the town. Next he said, "Hey, look at that glass elevator on the side of that building. Let's go ride on it." When we got off the elevator and headed to his truck without hearing those words I was disappointed, convinced that I had been imagining things.

We left Dallas and got on the interstate highway headed back home. In the center of the long bridge that crossed over Lake Ray Hubbard he blurted out, "Let's get married!"

1

I accepted his proposal. That was the beginning of an adventure that has never ended. I knew when I said "Yes" that night that I had just signed on for an adventure that would last a lifetime and boy was I ever right.

Five years later when Benny informed me he was going to going to be a Texas Game Warden, it was a game changer. I never dreamed I would be following him all over the state, from East Texas to West Texas and back home again to Hunt County, where he eventually retired.

For 25 years our lives....holidays, family meals, ball games, church, movie dates, vacations, and sleep were constantly being interrupted and cancelled because of sudden phone calls that required him to respond. Texas Game wardens are on call 24 hours a day, 365 days a year. Benny took that obligation seriously. We just had to suck it up and get used to the hectic lifestyle.

One thing I never did get accustomed to was the worry and stress over him getting called out into the night, possibly to a situation that might involve dangerous people with guns, or dangerous weather. Fortunately, with the exception of a few bumps and bruises, he always came home to me in one piece and standing upright. He had some harrowing stories to tell and I suspect that I still have not heard some of the worst of them to this day.

Thunder River contains many of these exciting stories. This book will give readers a good insight into the daily challenges faced by my husband and other Texas Game Wardens as they patrol the woods and waters.

–Kristi Richards

THUNDER RIVER

AT THE URGING of family, friends, and *Lone Star Law* fans I decided to write this book. My two previous books were received very well, so it was not a hard decision to sit down and go to work. Coming up with the content for a third book was also easy. As a Texas Game Warden for twenty-five years, I had enough stories to fill up a library with books. Most game wardens across the country do. The real challenge for me was coming up with a title. I always have thought that the title should give a reader some idea of what is contained inside the book. But whatever word or words were used should also make a potential reader want to pick up the book and have a look inside, out of curiosity. So it took some time—weeks, and then months, actually. Then one day as I was sitting alone in the woods, leaned against an oak, with a rifle lying across my lap, it came to me. I had the title I was looking for all along. I had had it for years. Thunder River.

Now stay with me while I explain what I'm talking about and where those two words come from. My whole life I have loved to hunt. My love for the pursuit of wild game began when I was just a young boy and continues today. I have always been a successful hunter. When I hit the field as a new game warden, all the neighboring wardens caught on to the fact that Benny knew where to go and what to do when he got there. Many of those wardens became close, trusted friends of mine.

One afternoon I was out on patrol when I spotted a flooded field near the Sulphur River. In that same field there were hundreds of green-headed mallards. One phone call later and I had permission to hunt the field the next morning. The next two phone calls were to two of my best friends and fellow game wardens, Rick Lane and Sean Reneau. Both of them wanted in on the duck hunt. That night the wind turned out of the north, and it began to snow. Just before daylight I met Rick and Sean at the edge of the field. We hurriedly constructed a makeshift brush blind. The three of us sat in the blind laughing and joking about the falling snow, waiting for the rising sun and the birds to come. And come they did. What happened next was the best duck hunt I had ever been on, and that's saying a lot. In a little over an hour, we were back at the truck with a three-man limit of mallards. We were all giddy about the hunt we had just experienced. At one point I bragged, "You guys better be glad y'all booked a hunt with this guide service." Rick responded, "Just what is the name of this guide service?" I thought for a second and said the first thing that came to my mind, "Thunder River Outfitters." I have no idea where the words came from, that's just what came out. Rick and Sean just laughed, and it became an inside joke amongst us. Afterward, anytime we had a good duck hunt, dove hunt, fishing trip, or got a big deer down, we would wink at each other and say, "Thunder River Outfitters strikes again."

Later, the "outfitters" part was dropped, and the term continued to evolve in its meaning. For example, if I built a barn that I was proud of, Thunder River Construction built it. If I unclogged a sink for my wife, Thunder River Plumbing cleared it. If I changed the oil on my old truck, Thunder River

Auto Repair did the work, and so on. In the years that followed, Thunder River became less of a joke and more of an actual place. I began to refer to my little piece of land as Thunder River. When I would go "10-7 at Thunder River Ranch" over the radio at the end of the day, the county dispatchers didn't know where I was talking about, I'm sure. However, every game warden that was listening knew exactly where I was.

Eventually times changed. Sean transferred to another part of Texas, and Rick retired, along with most of the other game wardens that I had worked with for so long. Younger guys took their place, and each time I would have to explain to the new warden about Thunder River. Those two words followed me to the end of my career. Even today, if I get a good buck or a pile of fish, I'll text an ole friend and write *Thunder River strikes again.*

So now you know the story of the title. I hope you will enjoy the stories on the pages behind it. God bless!

It Made a Great Handle

Sunrise on Thanksgiving morning found me doing what game wardens do in East Texas during that time. I was feverishly checking deer camps. Lots of hunters were in the woods, and I did my very best to check as many of them as possible. I started just before daybreak and patrolled all morning until noon. I took enough time to eat with the family, then I was right back at it. That pace didn't slow down until dark. A few citations had been written for minor stuff, but for the most part, it had been an uneventful day. Thanksgiving dinner was delicious, and I ate way too much, as always.

After visiting with relatives, I laid down for a nap, knowing my day wasn't even close to being over. I walked back out the front door around eight o'clock. I headed straight for an area known as Shawnee Creek Estates. I hadn't made it over to that part of the county in a few days, and I was eager to check it out. Shawnee was a large area of mostly uninhabited swampland. Partials of land there were separated into small thirty- and forty-acre blocks. Over one hundred different people owned land there. Hunting season brought in lots of folks during the holidays.

It was a very dark night as I drove through the front gate. I slow rolled past numerous camps, looking for hanging deer or hunters gathered around campfires. I was surprised at how

6

little activity I was finding. I pressed on and eventually found myself near the very back of the property. Whoa... what was that? Yep, there it was again. That all-too-familiar sight that warms a warden's heart. The glow of a spotlight was dancing around in the timber four hundred yards ahead. I turned out all my lights and slowly crept up to a locked gate.

As I got out of the truck, I heard the humming of an engine approaching. I climbed over the gate, walked past a trailer house, and up a trail to the west. Then I observed two four-wheelers riding side by side headed my way. The driver of one was steadily using a Q-beam to light up the woods. The pair, a man and woman completely unaware of my presence, drove right up to where I was standing in the trail. I turned on my flashlight to announce my arrival. Upon seeing me, the man jumped off and went to the back of his four-wheeler. The woman stayed seated on hers. Both had a rifle slung across one shoulder. Both were dressed completely in camouflage. Obviously deer hunters, I thought, and probably trying to get one at night.

I identified myself and asked the pair to lay their rifles down. They complied. She laid her lever-action across the front rack, and he laid his bolt-action across the seat. When I asked for hunting licenses, there was a pause, then they tried to tell me they had not been hunting, therefore did not need a hunting license. Of course, I wondered out loud, "What are the rifles for?"

"They are for hogs in case they get after us."

The guy was acting flaky and had some kind of weird facial twitch going on. I asked for his driver's license. He refused to show one and became belligerent and started cursing and complaining about harassment. He was now front and center on my radar. I noticed every time I tried to approach him, he would move to the other side of the four-wheeler. I finally had enough of that and told him to stop. I was way concerned about what was going through his mind and wanted to frisk him for weapons. I already had a couple of violations on him, and given his demeanor, a frisk was warranted. The man then suddenly did something very, very wrong in my mind. He turned his back to me and began reaching under his coat.

Let me set the stage. It was very dark. I was twenty miles minimum from the closest officer. I was behind a locked gate. I had two armed suspects, and one was larger than me and cussing as he fished for some unknown object under his coat. Nope... ain't happening. I wasn't going to get hurt or killed that night.

I grabbed the man and tried to handcuff him. This started a wrestling match. If he wanted to fight, I was all in, but I had no intentions of wrestling with him. I was looking for an opportunity to end this episode quickly. I found it in the form of his long ponytail hanging down from underneath his hat. It made a great handle. After using it to completely pull him off his feet backwards, I was perched on top of him. As all this was going on, I was also having to watch his woman. I had no idea what her response was going to be.

The struggle having ended, I removed his coat, looking for whatever it was he had been digging for. A glass pipe fell out of one of the coat sleeves. He was now under arrest. I stood the idiot up and began to handcuff him. As I did, I noticed something else. The four-wheeler he had been riding did not have a key in the ignition. I'll go ahead and say it turned out to have been recently stolen.

I marched the guy to my truck as the other followed. I loaded him up and prepared to travel to the Red River County jail in Clarksville, Texas. As I gave the woman instructions not to touch the stolen four-wheeler, her man began to plead with me to let him speak with her one last time before leaving. I consented and rolled down the passenger side window. They went through the whole "boo-hoo I love ya baby" routine, but there was some conversation that seemed out of place. He told her three times that he had dropped his knife and asked her to please be sure to go get it. Hell, I never saw any knife. Intuition kicked in. What did I miss?

I decided to make a quick trip back to the site of our struggle, and it was time well spent. A plastic bag full of cocaine about the size of a golf ball was found lying on the ground. Things just continued to go downhill for the guy, and charges just kept piling up. Just prior to my departing, dispatch advised me he was a felon. This information resulted in my taking every firearm I could locate at his camp. I booked him in the jail and filed a laundry list of charges. I then returned to the camp to seize the stolen four-wheeler. It was an interesting end to a very long day.

One month later I was sitting at my desk in my office doing paperwork when the phone rang. On the other end of the line was an ATF agent.

"Mr. Richards, are you the game warden that arrested Donald Jay Peabody?"

"Yessir, that would be me."

"Do you think I could possibly get a copy of your arrest reports?"

"That won't be a problem at all."

The agent went on to explain Peabody was being investigated by his agency for very serious weapons charges. He needed my reports to use as a basis for a search warrant. I agreed to provide the agent with all the information I had. I only asked one thing in return: if he would call me back and let me know how it all turned out.

The agent was a man of his word. A week or so later he called me back. Officers had arrested Peabody at his home in Collin County. Inside his home were dangerous drugs, numerous firearms, pipe bombs, and even a hand grenade. I was not surprised. It all goes to show you never know who is out there in those woods at night.

KUNG FU

EVERY WARDEN in any county has a spot. It's that spot where, when things get slow, he will visit that special area knowing that more than likely a violation can be discovered and a citation written. Texas Game Wardens were never under any quotas during my time in the field. But trust me, captains and majors paid attention to numbers. If your case numbers stayed too low for too long, it would probably be brought to your attention when it came evaluation time.

When I was stationed in Hunt County, my spot was Brushy Creek. Lots of trespass calls there. When I was in Red River County, my spot was Shawnee Creek Estates. Over one hundred hunting camps in a relatively small area. You can only imagine. In Dalhart it was Rita Blanca Lake. Every morning of the waterfowl season there brought in a whole new bunch of hunters to what was called "the firing line." All those spots generated a lot of calls and many citations over the years. However, of all the honey holes I had, one was head and shoulders above all the others when it came to issuing citations. The spillway at Cooper Lake. When I arrived there fresh out of the academy, the lake was full to capacity, and water was being released out of the spillway at a great rate.

Over the next five years nothing changed much. The lake stayed above normal level, and water continually flowed out the back of the dam. What is important to know about that

11

situation is that any time water was flowing out of the dam, large numbers of fishermen gathered there. Sometimes upward of two hundred or more on a good weekend. In addition to some illegal fishing, there was plenty of illegal hunting that went on there also. Great numbers of deer bedded down on the back of the dam each night, including some large bucks. I caught numerous poachers using spotlights there at night. Lastly, drug use was common in the parking lot at the spillway because of the remote location.

The dam at Cooper Lake is about three and a half miles wide. A two-lane highway runs across the top of the dam from one side over to the other. Below, at the base of the dam, another two-lane highway runs from the east side of the dam two miles and dead-ends into the parking lot at the spillway. The two highways are known as the upper road and the lower road, respectively. I spent hundreds of hours patrolling that dam during my time in Delta County. One tip I received, and the investigation that followed, highlights the type of work I did there that never seemed to let up. It all started with a phone call late at night from a pissed off fisherman. "Hey, what are y'all going to do about these Asians?"

"Whoa, whoa, whoa partner, slow down and tell me what's going on."

"These Asians are what's going on."

"What are they doing?"

"They are down here throwing these nets again."

The man went on to explain that a small group of Asian folks were using cast nets to indiscriminately take large numbers of game fish. This wasn't the only call. I had received a rash of calls over a short period of time. Each caller described the same group doing the same illegal activity, always at night. In each case, when I would show up, the violators were long gone. It was obvious I needed to get this stopped, and I needed a new approach. I called my neighboring warden, Kevin Davis, and explained my plan. A few days later, just after dark, we parked our patrol truck behind the Corps of Engineers' office on the upper road. A quarter mile walk and we were standing above the spillway below. We stepped over the metal guardrail and made our way down the back of the dam. At a spot halfway between the upper and lower roads, we stopped and sat down in the green grass of springtime. From our perch we had a clear view of the entire lower road, the parking lot, and the concrete wall from where most of the fishing was done. The plan was simple. Just wait, watch, and hope we picked the right night.

Over the course of three hours, we used binoculars to closely monitor the fishing activity at the spillway. We could have filed a few cases for snagging fish, but we were waiting for something much more flagrant. The moon rose high in the sky and, one by one, the fishermen began to reel in their lines and call it a night. About midnight we were bored to death. One or two holdouts sat on the rocks at the spillway below near the water's edge.

We were in the mood to give up when a set of headlights appeared at the east end of the lower road. Our interest perked up as the vehicle slowly made its way into the parking lot. It turned out to be a Ford van. After being parked, the side door slid open on the van and three men and one woman hopped out. With binoculars trained on the group, we watched as they unloaded several five-gallon buckets, shut the side door, and headed for the concrete wall. It was interesting that they didn't have any fishing poles in their possession. I didn't know if this was the group we were looking for, but I had a feeling we were about to witness a violation.

13

When they reached the end of the wall, they threw us a curve ball we hadn't expected. The three men walked out onto the wall; however, the woman turned uphill and began walking right toward us through the damp grass. Reacting quickly, we moved over about thirty feet and lay flat on the ground. Unbelievably, she walked to where we had been sitting, without seeing us. She stopped, turned, and just stood in front of us a few yards away. It was clear what was going on. She was sent to be a lookout for any law enforcement approaching from the lower road.

Meanwhile, the three men went to work. They pulled nets out of the buckets and started casting them over the side of the wall. Each net had a good load of fish when it came back over there top of the wall. They emptied the nets onto the concrete walkway and began putting fish into plastic bags. They appeared to be selective as they filled the bags. Some fish were left lying on the concrete as others were bagged up. Then they did something else unexpected. One of the men blew a whistle loudly. At the sound of the whistle the woman broke into a jog. She met the men at the wall, gathered all the bags of fish, and then made her way all the way to the top of the steep dam. The woman placed all the bags of fish on the ground under the guardrail and tied a white ribbon around the top of one of the wooden posts that supported the railing.

Kevin and I were astounded by what we were watching. These were definitely our suspects working in concert with each other like a well-oiled machine. This process repeated itself three times. Finally, they rolled up their nets and returned to the van. They had been at the spillway less than fifteen minutes. They left the parking lot without a care now, thinking if I showed up and stopped them, there would be no fish to explain. The suspects had come up with a pretty sneaky plan. They were on their way now to get on the upper road that crossed the dam. Then the next stop would be to retrieve the fifteen bags of crappie that had been hidden under the guardrail.

Kevin and I had about five minutes to prepare for their return. Kevin asked, "What do you want to do?" I replied, "Let's have some fun with these people." Kevin and I raced up to the top of the dam. I told Kevin, "Grab all these bags and follow me." Working quickly, Kevin and I gathered all the bags of fish and moved them about twenty yards over to a large junction box that housed electrical equipment. We hid the evidence and crouched out of sight behind the large metal box. We were both laughing to ourselves when the van slid to a stop next to the white ribbon wrapped around the post. From behind the box we could hear an excited conversation going on in some foreign language. I guessed it to be Mandarin. Peeking around both sides, we could see all the individuals frantically searching for the missing fish. They continued to look, and the conversation continued to get louder, until it appeared the woman might be assaulted by one of the men. We had seen enough. Kevin and I rolled out around both sides at a brisk pace. At a distance of twenty feet, we lit them up with flashlights. "State game wardens!" Complete silence fell over them.

"Howdy, folks, what's going on? Are y'all looking for something?"

There was no response from anyone.

"Did y'all lose some fish or something? We just happened to find some fish. Are they y'all's?"

There was still no response. At this point I walked over and grabbed two of the bags. I brought them back swinging them sarcastically out in front of me, one in each hand.

"Do y'all recognize these?"

They all began to chatter amongst themselves in that same foreign language. Attempts to communicate with them in English were greeted with shoulder shrugs and laughter. Finally, I told them the bad news.

"Y'all are all under arrest."

Then a funny thing happened. They all began to suddenly speak pretty good English, very good English. They wanted to know why they were going to jail. I explained everything thoroughly. Actually, to keep from impounding the van, the woman was released. Her three male partners in crime got to take a ride. Ninety crappie and three nets were confiscated.

The inmates at the county jail said it was the best fish fry they had ever had.

A Hot Tip

I **FOUND OUT EARLY** in my career that there is a lot of truth to the old saying "Sometimes it's better to be lucky than good." I always prided myself in my ability to catch a poacher. However, it was sometimes just a matter of being at the right place at the very right time.

Such was the case late one afternoon in early October near Cooper Lake in Delta County. The archery season had begun, and I was checking parking areas and any bow hunters going in or coming out of the woods. At one particularly wide spot near the end of a long dirt road, I located a couple of trucks parked near a public hunting area gate. Assuming they belonged to hunters, I decided to park my rig and wait awhile.

I had no more leaned the seat back and gotten comfortable than I noticed a young boy approaching on a bicycle. He looked to be about seven or eight years old. I didn't pay much attention and went to fiddling with something in the truck. It wasn't until the boy made his third lap around my truck that I perked up and started watching. A couple more laps and then he stopped in front of my truck and a staring contest began. I'm sure I must have chuckled a bit. It was obvious this kid had something on his mind. I finally motioned to him and said, "Hey, Junior, come here." He never hesitated. Before I could blink, he was at my driver's door with a big grin on his face. I asked him his name and gave him mine. After introductions were complete, he blurted out, "My daddy killed a big buck." Now I never hesitated. With a big grin on my face and with some enthusiasm I asked, "He did? Where?"

"Behind our house."

"When?"

"This morning."

"How big was he?"

"Twelve points!"

"Wow, that is big. What size gun did he shoot him with?"

"His .243."

Bingo.... Poor kid had just convicted his dad of hunting deer in a closed season with a rifle. I had no idea if the guy had actually killed the deer with a rifle. I guess I could have assumed he got it with a bow. I mean after all, it was archery season. However, I always put my suspicions first when asking questions. This time was no different. I will admit I felt slightly guilty knowing I was about to use this kid's words against his own father.

"I sure would like to see that big ole buck. Is your dad home?"

"Yeah, come on, follow me."

And off he went as fast as those short legs could pedal. I followed close behind around a corner, up a hill, and down a lane to a little wood-frame house. When we arrived, I lost any guilty feeling I'd had earlier. I knew the man who lived at this house. Delbert was his name and we were well acquainted. I quickly got out of my truck to catch up with the boy, who was going through the front door. After busting through, he said, "Daddy, the game warden is here, he wants to see the deer." Standing in the doorway, I was looking down at Delbert lying on the sofa, suddenly waking up from a nap.

"Howdy, Delbert. I hear you got yourself a really good buck."

"Uhhhh… uhhhh… yeah, I got a deer."

"Do you mind if I take a look at him?"

"Uhhhh… uhhhh… yeah, I guess so. What's all this about?"

"No problem, your son tells me you got a good buck, and I'd like to see it—and your hunting license, if that's OK."

Obviously trying to come with answers to questions he knew were coming, he led me to a shed in the backyard. Inside hung the severed head of a large twelve-point buck deer. To my surprise, a tag was taped to the antlers. At this point I asked to see his license. Conveniently, he could not seem to find his license. No matter. A quick phone call to our dispatch center in Austin, Texas, revealed everything I needed to know. He did indeed have a valid Texas hunting license. The problem was it had been purchased two hours prior to my arrival. So now I had the first confirmed violation. He did not have a license at the time he had killed the deer. This is the point where things went downhill and the lying started.

"Where did you kill this deer, Delbert?"

"In my pasture."

"You mean that two acres beside your house?"

"Yep."

"Do you really expect me to believe that?"

"I don't care what you believe."

"Where is the gun you shot the deer with?"

"I didn't shoot it with a rifle. I shot it with my bow."

"Can you show me a bloody arrow?"

"Never could find the arrow."

"Show me the guts and the hide."

"I already hauled it all off."

"Where to?"

"I don't even think I could find the place again."

"Oh really.... Wait here."

I called two other wardens I knew were not far away. I thought the sight of two additional game warden trucks pulling up into his yard might loosen his tongue. It didn't. With three wardens firing questions at him, he stuck to his original story that he killed a buck on his tiny piece of property, using a bow and arrow. In addition, he claimed our agency computers were completely wrong about the time in which he purchased his hunting license. Things started getting pretty heated between Delbert and the other wardens when I put up my hands and said, "Hold on, time out." Even as a rookie warden, I knew there was a big difference between what you know and what you can prove. And I knew also that to get a confession you sometimes had to make deals with the devil.

"Come take a walk with me, Delbert."

I led him to the back of my patrol truck away from the others. I then gave him one of my speeches I became famous for and offered him a deal.

"Delbert, I know and you know what happened here. I'm going to get to the bottom of this if it's the last thing on earth I do. I don't want to use your son against you, but I will. I promise you he will end up in tears, and it will be your fault. If you force me to prove what I know to be true, it's going to get really ugly. When I do prove it, I will file every charge I have against you, and that will ruin your Christmas for about the next three years. Do you want that? But I'll make you a deal. If you take me to the deer hide and show it to me... if you tell me the truth about this deer... I will write you one citation. I will not take the deer meat or your gun, and I will get these wardens off your ass and we will leave. So what's it gonna be?"

He took the deal. Delbert dropped his head for a few seconds and said, "Come on." He led me and the other two wardens to a fence line behind his house where we found a gut pile and a deer hide. Examining the hide, I found a perfectly round entry wound obviously made by a speeding bullet. Delbert confessed to shooting the deer on some church-owned property nearby. I had everything I needed now. The case was over.

True to my word, I issued one citation for hunting deer without a valid license. It was the most provable charge. I took the antlers and placed them in the bed of my patrol truck. Those antlers were the main motivation for killing the deer. The other two wardens and I drove away. Delbert didn't win, but he didn't lose as badly as he could have. I didn't win either. He got away with a few things. In the end, justice was served as best as I thought it could be served, all things considered.

I sometimes wonder if that little boy still talks to game wardens.

FRAT HOUSES

I HUNG UP the phone and headed out to Highway 24 south of Cooper. I had just been advised that another deer had been struck by a vehicle. When I arrived there, a large buck with an impressive set of antlers was lying dead beside the roadway. A few yards away a state trooper filled out his paperwork as a wrecker driver loaded up a mangled vehicle.

Something needed to be done about this, but what? Over the course of three months, I had responded to a half dozen collisions between cars and deer at this very spot. This half-mile stretch of highway ran along beside John's Creek. At one point the timber was very close to both sides of the highway. It was a deadly funnel for deer and other wildlife. The next day, trying to be proactive, I stopped by the local TXDOT office in town and asked to speak with someone about the possibility of getting some warning signs erected. I spoke to an engineer there about the situation out on 24. He agreed to have two signs put up but asked, "Do you think it will help?" I replied, "I don't know, but it can't hurt anything to try."

A week later two new large, yellow signs were put up with the words *Deer Crossing* below the silhouette of a running deer. I was proud to see the new signs. It gave me a good feeling knowing I was at least trying to do something. My good feelings didn't last very long, and neither did the two new large, yellow signs. About two weeks after being put up, they disappeared. Thieves decided they needed the signs more than the driving public did. I was pissed, but what could I do?

Fast-forward two months. I was up at the JP's office in the courthouse, filing some cases. The secretary said, "Oh, by the way, I have a couple of arrest warrants for you." It seemed a young man from Commerce decided not to honor his promise to appear when I had issued him two citations months earlier. Now the judge wanted me to go find him. I gathered the warrants and headed out the door. I took arrest warrants seriously and was very diligent in serving them. Once inside the patrol truck, I headed south. Using the information on a copy of the original citations, I was able to locate the address where the violator lived. To my surprise it turned out to be a frat house on the campus of Texas A&M University in Commerce, Texas. When I pulled up to the curb in front of the frat house, there were six guys playing sand volleyball in the yard. When I exited my truck and walked onto the lawn, I was greeted with nervous stares. I directed a question to no one in particular.

"Is Joshua here?"

One guy spoke up saying, "Yes sir, he is inside."

"Would you please take me to him?"

I followed the helpful frat boy into the living room, and I was followed by the other five. I was asked to wait. Down a hallway I heard a voice summoning young Joshua. As I waited, I noticed something very familiar hanging over the fireplace. Two large, yellow signs with the words *Deer Crossing* were displayed. "Well, well, well... looky here," I thought to myself.

At that moment Joshua walked out of the hallway and into the living room. I explained to him he had a total of four warrants. Two for the original violations, and two for failure to appear. He gave me no resistance or debate. Normally at this point, I would have escorted him out to my patrol truck before applying handcuffs. However, I changed things up a little for this situation. I wanted to make an impression on the other six sets of eyeballs looking on. After handcuffing Joshua, I told him to have a seat on the sofa. I then retrieved a chair from the kitchen. Using the chair I had placed at the base of the fireplace, I removed the two large, yellow signs from the wall above the mantle. With signs in hand, I turned to the frat boys and asked, "These are going with me... anybody got any questions?"

Complete silence filled the room. I collected the signs and my arrestee and left.

The following week the two large, yellow signs with the words *Deer Crossing* were back in place. They hung there for several years with no more problems except the occasional bullet hole.

HIT AND RUN

I'VE OFTEN SPOKEN about the dangers of game warden work and law enforcement generally. I spent almost twenty-five years wearing the blue badge of a Texas Game Warden. During those years I made hundreds of arrests, checked hundreds of camps, made thousands of traffic stops, spent thousands of hours in a boat, patrolled the Mexican border often, and responded to many natural disasters. I dealt with every type of hook and crook that society had to offer.

However... all of it almost never happened. Texas Game Warden was not my first law enforcement title. I began my law enforcement career as a patrol officer in Richardson, Texas, in 1993. An event that happened while on patrol there one afternoon almost brought my career and my life to a sudden end.

I had just finished my dinner break and climbed back into my patrol car in the north side of the city. As I was travelling back to my beat on the south side, I noticed two individuals standing beside a vehicle on the side of the roadway. The man and a woman appeared to be having a verbal confrontation with the driver of the vehicle. I slowed down and pulled up behind the vehicle to investigate. Upon seeing me, the man and woman turned and ran west across the grass median toward the service road. The driver of the vehicle punched the gas pedal and headed south on Central Expressway toward Dallas.

I had to make a quick decision. Should I chase the car or chase the people? If I chased the car, I might lose him in heavy traffic and/or cause an accident. Chasing the people on foot seemed like the better choice, and I was confident I could run them down with the Ford Crown Victoria I was riding in. I went to the next exit just ahead and left the expressway.

Cutting across three lanes of traffic on the service road, I entered a parking lot and pulled around behind a business complex. There they were. Reversing course, they ran back to the service road. I was right behind them within seconds. Having given up on escape, the pair stopped in the grass median between the service road and Central Expressway, almost the exact spot where the whole episode began.

I had stopped my patrol car in the far-left lane of the service road and gotten out. They gave me some story about being put out on the side of the road by the woman's father because of an argument about money. Both of them presented an Arkansas driver's license as identification. When asked, neither could explain why they ran from me. My guess was they needed to get rid of something in their possession before talking to any police. I gave instructions to "stay put and don't move." I needed to contact dispatch and do a computer check for warrants and criminal history. I got into my patrol car halfway with the door open. That is to say, I had one cheek on the seat and one cheek off. One foot inside and one foot on the pavement. The reason for this posture was to be ready if they tried to run away again. The roar of rush hour traffic was so bad I could not hear the dispatcher over the radio.

At this point, God was watching over me. I pointed my finger at the pair, as a second warning to stay put. I lifted my left leg, moved over on the seat, shut the driver's door, and lowered the driver's-side window. I reached over and picked up the microphone. I lifted it toward my mouth to speak, and that was the last thing I remember.

When I regained consciousness, I was lying on an emergency room bed at Parkland Memorial Hospital in Dallas. Beside my bed stood my wife Kristi, my mom, and my patrol sergeant, Bob Williams.

Was this real? Was I dead? I wasn't sure what was going on. What I was sure of was the gash in my head and the terrible nausea brought on by a severe concussion. Sergeant Williams began to explain to me that I was struck from behind by a drunk driver.

I asked, "Well, did y'all catch the guy?"

"Oh, yeah... it took a while, but we got him."

A very drunk Mexican national, in the country illegally, had rammed my patrol car at seventy miles per hour without ever hitting his brakes. The impact turned my patrol car into an accordion and knocked it across the grass median and partially into southbound Central Expressway. The uninjured drunk fled the scene on foot, leaving me for dead. Lots of witnesses began flooding the dispatch center with 911 calls about an officer hurt badly in an accident. Dispatch immediately started protocol and conducted a roll call over the radio. When unit 271 didn't respond, they knew it was me and rolled out the fire department and an ambulance. Unbelievably, the responding fire engine was commanded by Captain Mackie Don Babers. Captain Babers was my father-in-law. I can only imagine his surprise when he pulled open that door and saw me slumped over and bleeding. He personally helped load me in an ambulance and rode with me to the hospital.

The drunk proceeded to find a quiet place to hide and sleep behind an office building. A good officer and a good dog located his sorry ass about an hour later. In the end, I spent a couple of days in the hospital but made a full recovery, no worse for the wear. I was back on duty in less than a week. The drunk Mexican bonded out of jail and to my knowledge was never heard from again.

I learned several lessons that afternoon: Law enforcement is dangerous business. Never let your guard down. We are not guaranteed anything. You can be here one moment and gone the next.

GUT FEELINGS

FIELD GAME WARDENS learn to expect the unexpected. They get all kinds of calls at all times of the day and night. They learn to keep their trucks stocked with equipment and a dependable boat at the ready at all times. Sadly, some calls they receive have a predictable outcome. Wardens who have been around awhile can usually make those predictions based on years of experience. Drownings are those types of calls. When a warden receives a call about an overdue fisherman and then finds his truck and trailer at the ramp and an empty boat drifting nearby, it's a good bet that that call won't end well. Many times hunters are the focus of missing persons calls.

Warden Daniel Roraback and I had a string of such calls while I was stationed in Red River County. Just after dark one afternoon I received a call from a woman near Dallas who advised her husband was supposed to have returned home the prior day from a hunting trip. She went on to explain his phone was going straight to voice mail. I gathered all the information I could and then gave Daniel a call. We met at the sheriff's office in Clarksville and headed up to an area known as the North Woods. Using the information the woman had provided, we were able to locate the missing hunter's truck parked in front of a hunting cabin. We expected to find the man inside the cabin. No such luck. Everything was in order inside the cabin. No signs of foul play and no indication of where the hunter was. We did not find a hunting rifle inside the cabin or the vehicle. We assumed the guy was somewhere nearby, still in the woods.

At this point I got one of those gut feelings. In the darkness, Daniel located boot prints in the soft mud behind the cabin. The tracks led across a small creek and down a trail into thick timber. Using flashlights we slowly followed the tracks for about two hundred yards. Then I got a glimpse of something metallic ahead. It was the legs of a tall deer stand leaning against a big oak. Our missing hunter was lying lifeless on the ground at the base of the tree. The local justice of the peace was summoned to the scene. The local deputies made the death notification by phone. A later autopsy revealed the man had died of a massive heart attack, which had caused him to fall from the stand.

Not many weeks later, another missing-person call came in. This time it was a worried housewife in Mount Vernon who called to report her husband had not returned from a trip to the family farm in Annona. She said he had told her he needed to do some shredding and would be back home for dinner. As before, the woman could not make phone contact with her husband.

We arrived at the farm at 10:00 p.m. The missing man's truck was sitting beside the barn with the tailgate down. A few hand tools lay on top of the tailgate. We searched the barn from top to bottom and found no signs of anyone. The tractor was missing, so we stood silently and just listened for a few moments to see if we could detect an engine running in the distance. Nothing but complete silence.

Daniel and I walked south from the barn and noticed fresh-cut grass and weeds and tracks made by tractor tires. We guessed at a possible direction of travel and headed west on foot. We hadn't walked too far when I noticed a red reflection in the distance at a fence row. It turned out to be a red reflector on the back of the tractor we were looking for. The tractor, with shredder attached, was sitting against a tree and had some front-end damage. This indicated to us it was moving forward when it struck the tree. The engine had died with the tractor in gear.

At this point I got another one of those gut feelings. The missing man was nowhere in sight. Daniel and I began walking counter-clockwise around the field, following the edge of the cut grass. We hadn't made a complete lap when we found him. His lifeless body lay on the ground in front of us. His wounds indicated he had been thrown from the tractor or had gotten off for some unknown reason and was run over by the shredder. Again the justice of the peace was called.

I hope I never get another one of those gut feelings again for as long as I live.

YIPPEE-YI-YO-KIYAY

I'VE ALWAYS BEEN on board when it came to something new, especially if it was fun and exciting. So, when Warden Chris Fried invited me to patrol off horseback while checking turkey hunters on opening day, I was in.

Actually, we had patrolled off horseback about two months before. Call it a test run. I had ridden the horse he had picked out for me, so we had some history together. He was a little ornery at times, but I had no concerns. That spring morning was clear and bright with a chill in the air as we started unloading horses out of the trailer. Chris had a wide smile on his face, and his enthusiasm for the work ahead was obvious. We slung our saddles onto the horses and cinched everything up tight as the sun peeked up over the horizon. It was a beautiful morning and a great day to be a Texas Game Warden. I missed my first clue that things might change.

Chris untied my horse and took the lead rope. I asked, "What are you doing? Am I riding him?"

"Yeah, he is yours, but let's get some energy out of him. I'm going to lunge him a bit."

Standing in the middle of the road, Chris ran my horse in six or seven big circles as I looked on. I never gave it a second thought. Hell, they were his horses. He knew what to do, right?

32

"That ought to do it," he said as he handed off the lead rope. Just as if I had done it a thousand times, I wrapped the reins around the saddle horn, put my left foot in the stirrup, and pulled myself up and halfway over. It was about the time my right leg went over the saddle that I realized that I was airborne. My flight was short, and the stop was sudden and painful. I had been tossed about ten feet in the air and landed on my right side in the middle of a gravel road. As I lay motionless on my back, I could see my horse running away, bucking wildly as he went. Chris was giving chase from atop his horse.

I knew I was hurt but how severely? I did a quick evaluation. I was breathing. I could feel my feet and move my arms. So I wasn't dead, and I wasn't paralyzed. I rolled over onto my knees and elbows. No bones broken, I guessed. Chris came riding back up, towing my horse behind his.

He bailed off and asked, "Do I need to call an ambulance?"

Hesitantly I said, "I don't know, give me a minute."

Slowly and painfully, I rose to my feet. The pain in my right side was excruciating. But I will admit that a close second was the pain I felt from embarrassment from being thrown off my horse.

Over the next ten minutes it became clear that I was going to live. I downplayed the pain I was feeling because I knew Chris had really looked forward to this day and this ride.

Then I did a really dumb thing. Chris asked me if I was good. I told him that yes, I was ready to go ahead and ride. I was not ready to go ahead and ride. Not even close.

Chris made a change in horse assignment. He climbed up in the saddle on what had been my horse for the day. He ran that horse up and down the road until its tongue was hanging out.

"He won't do that shit again."

33

I climbed on top of his horse, and off we went into the timber. The pain wasn't too bad as long as we were riding on level ground. However, every time the horse stumbled or had to jump across a creek, the pain became almost unbearable. We checked a few hunters but really didn't have much luck catching any violators.

At the end of that long day, I was never so glad to crawl into my patrol truck and head home. My wife had to help me undress and get into the bathtub. I spent the next week sleeping in a recliner in our living room. It was the only way I could get comfortable enough to sleep. I got progressively better very slowly. But every time I sneezed or had to cough, I just felt like it would be better if I just went ahead and died.

It was about six months before I felt good again. I don't think that injury to my ribs ever fully healed. I vowed to never get on the back of another horse, but I broke my word. I've been back in the saddle several times since.

SMASH

VERY LATE ONE NIGHT I was headed home after a long patrol near the community of Lydia in Red River County. As I drove along Highway 44, I suddenly caught a glimpse of something flying toward my truck. In the blink of an eye, whatever it was hit the passenger-side door with a loud thud. It sounded like someone had hit my truck with a softball.

I drove on about a mile before curiosity got the best of me. I turned around and drove back to the spot, and there it was, lying in the road: the lifeless body of some small bird, deader than a doornail. I pulled up beside the bird to get a better look. At first I thought it was a bobwhite quail. It was the same color and about the same size. But then I saw those hairy legs and sharp little talons. I knew then it was some kind of owl.

I got out of the truck, and on closer inspection I determined it was an eastern screech owl. Being very cold, I jumped back into the truck, holding the little hooter. I sat in the driver's seat with him cradled in my hands, sad that such a beautiful creature had to die in such a terrible way. I decided to take him home to show my daughter Kaitlin, who had a soft spot for injured animals.

However, just before I put the truck in gear, I thought I felt the owl quiver. What's this? Signs of life? I didn't know what else to do, so I blew into his face. Yeah, I definitely felt something then. I blew into his face a second time, and to my surprise, the little owl threw open his eyes wide, opened his beak, and took a deep breath. I had just witnessed a miracle.

My excitement was short lived, though, because the owl decided to give me a semiliquid gift that landed square in my lap and ran down the side of my leg onto the truck seat. I would have thought that this reaction would have happened immediately after the owl smashed his head into the side of my truck. Perhaps this was his way of telling me I had bad breath. Anyway, I wrapped him in a raincoat and laid him in the back seat, then headed home. I stopped in Cuthand long enough to check on him. He was still hanging in there but didn't look too good. I decided that if the little guy made it through the night, I would name him Smash.

I also planned to take him to the bird rehabilitator in Mount Vernon the next day to give him the best chance possible for survival. At the house, Kaitlin took one look at the owl and immediately adopted him. She wrapped him in a towel, placed him in a plastic garbage can, and covered it with an old shirt. After a few words of encouragement, she wished him a good night.

Early the next morning, Kaitlin woke me up and, together, we uncovered the trash can to check on Smash. When the shirt was taken off, out popped Smash. He was wide eyed and ready for anything. He flew around the room twice before landing on an opened closet door. Our housecat was sitting a few feet away licking his lips. This was the first good look I'd gotten of Smash in the daylight. He was about six inches tall, and three inches of that was yellow eyeballs. He looked healthy and no worse for the wear. No need for the bird rehabilitator.

I decided to leave him alone, perched on the door for the remainder of the day. We turned off all the lights in the room and spread out some newspapers below him in case he delivered anymore unwanted gifts. Later that day, at sunset, Kaitlin and I managed to sneak up behind Smash and grab him. We took him out into the yard and pitched him up into the air. Smash took flight and soared up onto a big limb in an oak tree near the house. We spent several minutes watching him as he spent several minutes watching us. It was humorous to see his head spinning around in circles as the dogs ran around the yard. Finally, we bid Smash good luck and farewell.

As I walked away, I stopped and looked back one more time. Maybe I was imagining things, but I could have sworn I saw that owl wink at me. Nah, surely not.

THE MOST DANGEROUS HOLE

EVERYONE KNOWS Texas Game Wardens work alone much of the time. It has a lot to do with the math. There are 254 counties in Texas that are patrolled by approximately five hundred field wardens; 268,596 square miles is a lot of ground to cover. Either by choice or county assignment, Texas Game Wardens routinely show up to calls all by themselves. I actually enjoyed working alone. I didn't have to consult with anyone about decisions I made. Plus, I was a night owl. A lot of guys didn't share my enthusiasm for all-nighters. However, working alone carried risks. It is dangerous working without backup, and for a game warden you can double that risk.

I backed into a large hay barn that was open on three sides on a hill. This hiding spot gave me a clear view of a long stretch of highway and a dirt road that paralleled it a half mile to the west. The Red River and Oklahoma were just over the hill to my right. It was a great spot for night hunters because of the large number of deer in the area and the seclusion. It was way out in the sticks, as they say. I spent the time listening to an FM station and looking for the occasional falling star. Sometime past midnight I saw the glow of approaching headlights to my left. Once the vehicle came into view, it kept a steady pace, so I didn't think it to be a night hunter at first. That all changed quickly.

The vehicle was a truck, and it turned onto a dirt road that wound around and ran parallel to the stretch of highway I was watching. In reality, I knew the second the truck turned onto that dusty road that someone, or everyone, in it was going to be receiving a citation or going to jail that night. There was simply no good reason to be on that road at that time unless you were up to something nefarious.

I started my patrol truck and, with the lights turned off, rolled out to the highway. I blocked the dirt road where it intersected with the highway in case the truck turned around and came back. I climbed into the bed of my truck with a good pair of binoculars. There they were, driving slowly down the road, shining spotlights out both sides of the truck. The truck was about a half mile away when it crossed the ditch and entered a soybean field. Through my glasses I could see deer running in all directions. The truck drove to the center of the field, and that's when the shooting began. A half dozen shots rang out. I clearly saw two deer hit the ground. That's all I needed to see.

A little puzzled and a little concerned about the number of shots I had heard in a such a short period of time, I climbed back into my rig and headed down the dirt road with lights still off. The illegal hunters had also turned off all their lights. When I got to the spot where I thought the truck had crossed over into the field, I did likewise. I drove slowly at first, but when I saw a flashlight begin bouncing around in the field, I rushed toward it. Fifty yards from the suspect vehicle, I lit them up. I turned on headlights, overhead spotlight, and all my red and blues. I was not prepared for what my lights revealed. In the bed of the truck stood three men all holding M4-type rifles. Behind the truck two more men were dragging a buck deer. They, too, were carrying M4-type rifles. Holy shit!

I drove right up in the middle of potentially the most dangerous hole I had ever dug for myself. Time to start digging myself out quickly, but how? There were two options as I saw it. I could drive away and create distance or get out and put the fear of God Almighty in all of them. I opted for plan B.

I exited my truck with my M4 rifle. Walking briskly toward them, rifle at the ready, I shouted, "Everybody get on the ground now, or I will kill every last one of you!"

As the men in the back of the truck got out and lay on the ground, I was still yelling some very strong language that I won't repeat. I had no intention of shooting anyone unless I had to, but I wanted to create a lot of doubt in their minds. The two men who had been dragging the deer slowly walked over to the other three and lay facedown beside them. This was still a very dangerous situation. Outnumbered five to one in the dark, I had no idea what was going to happen. Still barking out warnings, I began to collect rifles and drag them a safe distance away. As I did, one of the men said, "Warden, I need to tell you something."

"I don't need to hear a damn thing you have to say. Stay down."

A couple of rifles later, he tried again.

"Can I tell you something?"

"No! Shut up and be still."

Having removed all the rifles I could locate, I walked to the truck to inspect the interior. There were no more guns, but there was a huge surprise. A teenage girl sat quietly in the back seat. I was lucky on this night. These were not bad men willing to do me harm. At this point I was confused about the girl but felt safe enough to pull things back a notch and de-escalate the situation. I walked over to the men and in a lighter tone said, "OK, what is it you want to tell me?"

"Uhhhhh, sir... we are all prison guards."

I just stood speechless for a moment.

"Prove it."

All the men began pulling out badges and presenting them to me. Unbelievable... I now knew I had a big mess on my hands. These guys had just committed felonies right in front of me. Their very careers were now hanging in the balance. I almost felt guilty for catching them. As it would turn out, the two deer killed at night were not even their biggest problem. At that very moment, it began to rain cats and dogs. I knew we needed to get out of that field before it got muddy. I instructed the men to load the dead deer into the back of my truck as I loaded all their rifles into my back seat. I then collected driver's licenses from all the men and got a verbal ID on the sixteen-year-old girl. Standing in the driving rain, I told all of them to load up in their truck and follow me to the sheriff's office in town, where we would sort everything out. On the way to the jail, I called my dispatcher and briefly told her my situation. I also asked her to do a computer check on the name and date of birth of the girl.

This is where things got worse for the five men. About five minutes later the dispatcher called me back with disturbing news. She advised the sheriff's office had been looking for that young girl for several days since she had been reported missing. This was suddenly way above my pay grade. My next phone call got my captain out of bed. I explained to Captain Skip McBride all that had transpired. To his credit, Skip just said, "Benny, I'll leave it up to you to do what you think is best and stand behind you. But you deal with the wildlife part of it, and turn the rest over to the sheriff."

"10-4, Boss."

When I arrived at the sheriff's office followed by the five men and the girl, I was met by a deputy and an investigator. I explained to everyone that I was going to issue all the men citations and release them rather than put them in jail. The investigator stated, "That's all fine, but they ain't going anywhere until we find out why this girl is with them."

I issued citations to all five men and returned all of their rifles to them. I was able to donate the two deer over the phone. Then I drove away into the night. All the fines were collected over the next few days by the justice of the peace. To this day, however, I do not know what became of the situation with the teenage girl and the guards.

NAP TIME

I'VE ALWAYS BEEN a roamer. Late in my game warden career I began to become bored with the same old thing every day. Same old country, same old faces, same old types of calls. At that same time I was aware the clock was ticking on my career. I was no longer a young man and had only so many years left. I began to volunteer for any assignments anywhere in Texas. I was looking for any opportunity to stretch my legs and see more of the state while in uniform. I did numerous weeklong tours to the Mexican border. There, I got to patrol an area over five hundred miles wide from McAllen to the Big Bend region. I also did a couple of tours in the panhandle during the open pheasant season. There were other short tours to various lakes spread out across the land.

In November of 2018 I was itching to see far West Texas. I had spent some time there and loved those mountains. I asked my supervisor for permission to patrol out there. After he got the green light from the captain in El Paso, I started packing my bags. I was told to coordinate with the new rookie warden there, who had hit the field just a few weeks prior to my arrival. I had an agenda as I drove west. Far West Texas had a reputation amongst field wardens as a dead area where there was nothing much to do. I knew from personal observations that most wardens assigned there spent most of their time in El Paso working traffic and patrolling city parks. The same wardens just put their time in and then transferred at the first opportunity. Let it be known there is not a square inch of Texas that is a dead area for a warden who cares enough to get out there and work. I meant to prove what could be accomplished out there by a highly motivated man with a badge.

I met Ryan Svehla and another young warden as they ate lunch at a café in Van Horn. After introductions, I sat quietly and listened to the ramblings of two rookie game wardens. The inexperienced but enthusiastic conversation took me back to the days when I was fresh out of the academy. After lunch Ryan and I parted ways with the other warden. At Ryan's house, I parked my truck and jumped into his. Ryan wasted no time setting the stage for the rest of the day.

"Hey, I'm new here, so I really don't have a plan. What do you think we should do?"

I laughed at his honesty and pointed north. "Take me to those mountains."

In the distance the Guadalupe Mountains could be seen against a beautiful blue skyline. The thirty-mile trip allowed Ryan and me to get acquainted. I found him to be a jolly fellow with an admirable quality: he wanted to learn all he could. Near the tiny town of Dell City, we made a few back roads just to get a feel for the area. I finally spotted an irrigated alfalfa field that lay in the shadow of the mountains to the east.

"OK Ryan, there's our spot."

In the middle of the field, twenty head of mule deer were bedded down, along with a dozen pronghorn antelope.

I said, "We need to find a spot to hide."

"Why, what are we going to do?"

"We are going to wait on somebody to come along and blast one of those deer."

"Really? Do you think somebody will?"

"If I was a betting man, I would put good money on it."

The area was flat, with no cover in any direction. A stack of irrigation pipe placed at the south side of the field near a berm provided the obstacle I hoped would hide us just enough from the highway that ran parallel to the field. After backing the truck in place, I leaned my seat way back and told Ryan simply, "Wake me up if you see anything."

"How long do you want me to sit here?"

"Long enough for me to get a nap."

At that point I dozed off into a blissful sleep. I'm not sure how much time had passed by before my slumber was interrupted by Ryan shaking me.

"Hey, wake up. They're here."

I sat up to see a black SUV sitting beside the highway at the north end of the field. Two minutes later both doors swung open on the SUV. Two men got out and went to the rear of the vehicle and opened the back hatch. Looking through binoculars, Ryan could see the men removing scoped rifles. At this point they were done, they just didn't know it. Cases could be filed based solely on what we had already witnessed, but it was about to get better. The two rogue hunters walked to the edge of the field and got down on their hands and knees and began crawling toward the deer still bedded in the center of the large field.

I told Ryan, "Start the truck, let's go."

"Won't they see us?"

"It don't matter now, let's go."

We slowly came out from behind the stack of pipe and slow rolled toward the highway as the hunters continued to crawl. They never saw us. They were too honed in on the herd of deer three hundred yards in front of them. Ryan pulled up beside their vehicle and killed the engine, and we got out with two sets of binoculars. Leaning over the hood of the SUV, we had a front-row seat to what was about to unfold. They closed the gap to about 150 yards before the deer stood up. That caused all hell to break loose.

The two men opened fire, and deer immediately began to hit the ground. Two does fell, and a third deer that was obviously hit struggled to get to the fence line as lead continued to fly. The guys had just compounded their problems and tripled their fines. These were mule deer does they were killing. Bucks were the only legal deer, and there was not an antler anywhere in the field.

I told Ryan, "Let's go. I'll drive."

I jumped behind the wheel of the patrol truck. After clearing the ditch, I drove across the field to within twenty-five yards of the first hunter, where I told Ryan, "Get out." I then continued driving across the field, attempting to catch up to the second hunter, who was now chasing the wounded deer. Still totally unaware of our presence, the man raised his rifle and fired another shot as I pulled up. I exited the truck and yelled, "Drop that damn gun on the ground, now!" I had had enough of the shooting.

Startled, the man laid his rifle down and walked to me. The charges had stacked up quickly: Hunting from a vehicle on a roadway. Hunting without landowner's consent. Taking antlerless deer in a closed season. Exceeding the annual bag limit of mule deer.

After the two hunters were brought back together, Ryan checked licenses as I followed a blood trail into the brush, trying to locate the wounded deer. Ryan made a phone call to the landowner. These guys were looking at possible felony charges. However, the landowner didn't want to pursue the hunting without landowner's consent or the trespassing. In the end, we confiscated the deer and handled the whole situation with multiple Class C citations. When we turned the two men loose and sent them on their way, Ryan was giddy. He had just made his first deer cases as a warden, and they were good ones, too. It's not often a warden gets to stand and watch as a violator commits a serious crime.

That weekend proved to be very productive and obviously had an impact. I was invited back the next year. Twelve months didn't change much; there was still work to do around Dell City. I caught two college students red-handed. They had killed two large mule deer bucks using a spotlight at midnight in a wheat field.

West Texas is not a dead area for Texas Game Wardens... at least not this one.

A LONG SHOT

AS A YOUNG FATHER I looked forward to the day when my son could accompany me on my hunting trips. Once that day came, Erik was my best hunting buddy. Around the age of six he started tagging along—without a gun at first, but it wasn't too long before he learned to shoot, and shoot well. The rifle I taught him to hunt deer with was a Remington, bolt-action, chambered in .243 caliber. It wasn't a fancy rifle, and it was topped with an inexpensive scope. Between the two of us, many deer were harvested with that old rifle.

One afternoon I had decided to call it a day early and do some hunting with Erik. I picked him up after school and we headed for Huddleston's, a convenience store in Bogata. Snacks and drinks in hand, we then headed out to the prairie north of town. The property we hunted was a large tract of land I had leased from the Cherokee Nation up in Oklahoma. It was rolling prairie with CRP grass abundant and scattered trees. A canvas pop-up blind was what we used for concealment on a fence row. Prior to the season starting, I had shredded shooting lanes through the tall grass. It was a great setup.

That afternoon turned out to be slow hunting. We passed the time watching the acrobatics of hawks as they chased field mice. We also had a brief visit from a bobcat that strolled by.

48

At five o'clock the sun had gone down behind the trees, and we threw in the towel. We left the blind and started the long walk back to the truck. I followed behind my son as we made our way along a fence row. Suddenly, he stopped and pointed to the east.

"Look, Dad... deer."

I spotted them. Five deer were grazing in a field just under the horizon. In the fading light, I couldn't tell much about the animals other than the fact that they were deer.

I said, "Let me see the rifle."

Taking the rifle, I used the scope to examine the small herd. To my surprise there was a large ten-point buck in the bunch.

"Oh wow, Erik, there's a big buck down there."

Upon hearing this he began to ask me to take a shot. I knew better. I tried to reason with him by saying that I couldn't make an accurate shot at that range and might cripple a good deer. He was persistent, and his request turned into a plea. I thought about it. My son and I had been hunting hard for two weeks without anything to show for our efforts. I didn't want Erik to become discouraged and begin to associate hunting with failure. This kid needed to see a deer on the ground.

"Ok then, I'll try."

I walked over to a bois d'arc fence post and rested the rifle across the top. I made my best guess at where to hold the crosshairs inside the scope. With shaky confidence I slowly squeezed the trigger. The recoil and muzzle flash caused me to blink.

Just a split second after the sound of the shot, Erik began to excitedly proclaim, "You got him... you got him!"

In the distance I could see only four deer running away, that was true. However, I tried to tamp down Erik's expectations by saying, "I don't think I got him."

He sternly disagreed, "I saw him fall down."

I had such little confidence in the shot that I walked to my truck and left the rifle inside. The two of us walked in a straight line to where the deer had been standing when I fired the shot. I needed to prove to my son the deer was gone. I found out just minutes later that I was the one who was wrong. As we neared the spot, something began to thrash about in the grass ahead. It was him, the buck. The bullet had found its mark and had broken the animal's back, partially paralyzing him.

I turned to Erik and said, "Listen to me closely. Sit down right here and wait on me. I have to go get the gun. Whatever you do, don't approach that deer."

He just nodded his head in understanding. I turned and ran to the truck and returned with the rifle I never should have left behind. I finished the job. The kid was right all along and super excited to remind me of it.

The distance turned out to be a little farther than I thought: 498 paces. I won't take a lot of credit for a skilled shot. More likely just pure luck.

ARE YOU GOING TO LET OUR PRISONER ESCAPE?

CHRIS AND I had been subjected to a pretty good cussing on the way to the jail. We just ignored it and wrote it off as ramblings of an idiot. We had snagged this guy at the City of Greenville Municipal Lake. When we checked him fishing, he was in possession of a sizable amount of meth and a stolen handgun. His Saturday night was now going to be spent in lockup. We booked him in and completed the required paperwork, then left without further incident.

Exactly seven days later Chris called me up. "Hey, do you want to hit the Greenville Lake again?" I, of course, was all in. The Greenville city lake during the summer was a hotbed of activity after the sun went down. There were some fishing violations to be found, but more commonly, drug use was the most frequent offense. Either way, we were always assured of writing citations and possibly making arrests.

Chris and I had no more than pulled into the entrance of the lake when we saw two bicycles lying in the roadway. A short distance away, under the moonlight, a lone figure could be seen fishing off of a concrete culvert. The culvert ran underneath the roadway and emptied into the lake on both sides. I killed the engine and we got out of the truck. Chris went to move the bicycles out of the road, and I went to contact the fisherman. It turned out to be a young boy fishing alone. I struck up a conversation with the twelve-year-old. He told me he and his uncle had ridden the bicycles to the lake from his home in Greenville. At that very moment I began to hear Chris barking out commands to "Drop it... drop it!"

A male figure had suddenly walked up out of the darkness when Chris was moving the bicycles. After Chris was confronted by the subject, he attempted to pat him down for weapons. The subject pulled something out of his pants pockets and was holding it in his left hand. When I reached Chris I immediately realized why he was attempting to pat the guy down. It was the very same guy we had arrested seven days prior. Thirty-year-old Xavier Lee Nelson was his name.

Chris had a grip on Nelson's T-shirt and right wrist as they spun in circles in the center of the dirt road. I grabbed Nelson's left wrist with one hand and retrieved my handcuffs with my other hand. At the sight of my handcuffs Nelson dropped the object he had been holding and started fighting us like a wild animal. He was able to break free from our grip; he ducked his head and started throwing wild haymakers. Chris was hit squarely in the face with one punch. Then I got hit in the side of the head, which made my ears ring and caused me to drop my cuffs. This is where he made his big mistake.

I bull-rushed him and tackled him to the ground. Chris got caught up in the melee and ended up on the bottom of the pile. However, he was able to roll out quickly and get back up on his feet. As I was sitting on top of Nelson now, we traded blows until he finally laid his arms out to his side and said, "OK, I give up."

Having thoroughly convinced him that he was fighting a losing battle, I rolled him over and Chris applied the handcuffs. I pulled Nelson from the ground and escorted him over to my patrol truck. Pressing him against the front of the truck, I said, "You plant your butt on that bumper and don't move."

Now Chris and I checked each other for injuries. Finding nothing too serious, we then began to search the ground for my missing handcuffs and whatever Nelson had dropped on the ground. We had searched for about a minute when I heard something peculiar. I looked up to see Nelson running away with his hands handcuffed behind his back. I shouted, "Hey Chris, are you going to let our prisoner get away?" Chris looked up and, in disbelief, began to give chase. I will admit to laughing my ass off watching Chris run down the escaping criminal. It took about a quarter mile.

By the time Chris returned with our guy in tow, I had found my handcuffs and located a small plastic baggie of meth. It was about this time that Chris and I realized we had a slight problem. We had forgotten about the kid. The nephew of Nelson had been standing quietly off to the side, observing everything that went down. We needed to and were ready to go to the jail but couldn't leave the juvenile to fend for himself. I called the Greenville Police Department to ask for assistance. When their officers arrived, I asked them to transport Nelson to jail and hold him until we could get there. Chris and I loaded two bicycles into my truck and drove them and the kid to his home a few miles away. After getting him home and explaining everything to his mother, we left, in route to the jail.

We never made it. Instead, a Greenville PD unit called on the radio and advised that the jail personnel said they wouldn't take Nelson until he had been cleared by a physician at a hospital. Well hell. So we met the Greenville officer in the parking lot at Hunt Regional Medical Center. He was complaining that his shoulder was broken. Chris and I were led into an examination room, along with our arrestee. When nurses tried to get information from him, Nelson would only curse them. Fifteen minutes went by before a doctor entered the room. Now Nelson put his racism on full display. He refused to let the doctor examine him and stated, "I want to see a black doctor." The doctor replied, "I am the physician on duty. Will you let me examine you?" Nelson refused and said, "Keep your white-ass hands off of me." The doctor attempted to assess any visible injuries while being verbally tormented. Finally, having had enough of insults, the doctor looked at Chris and me and said, "In my opinion, his injuries are minor." He signed a couple of documents, turned, walked out of the room, and closed the door behind him. That was good enough for us. We scooped up Nelson and returned him to jail, where he was booked in for the second time in one week. He faced numerous felony charges.

However, sometimes justice is a hard thing to find. A few months later, Nelson was given credit for time served and let out of jail. He was not prosecuted for any of the felony charges, including the attack on us. Is it any wonder police officers often just feel like giving up?

HE BIT ME

MY ABILITY TO get into shit, both on and off duty, was legendary amongst game warden captains and majors. I never went looking for trouble, not once. But then again, I never shied away from it either, not once. As a peace officer and public servant, I considered myself to be like a sheepdog watching over the flock. Sheepdogs don't take days off. I can think of a dozen incidents that happened to me when I was off duty. One of those incidents stands out above all the rest.

Let me give you some background. I bought my son, Erik, a skateboard on his seventh birthday. He took to that skateboard like a duck takes to water. He was a natural. It wasn't long before that kid was doing tricks uncommon for his age. His love of skateboarding led our entire family to seek out venues for Erik to apply his new talent. Over a six year period we travelled all across the country, visiting skate parks as we went. From Texas to New Mexico, Colorado, Wyoming, Nebraska, Kansas, Utah, Oklahoma, and Arkansas, he skated and competed at every skate park we could find.

Now anyone who knows anything about skate parks knows they can attract the dregs of society. Not always, but very often. However, outside of a couple of minor incidents up in Colorado, our family just got to spend time watching our son do something he loved to do and was very good at. We just ignored some of the idiots that would inevitably show up.

When Erik was in the seventh grade, we were living in a small community not far from Paris, Texas. He came home one day from school and told us at the dinner table about a skateboarding competition being held in Paris that weekend. Not much to discuss... we were going to be there. Saturday morning came and we drove to the skate park in downtown. Erik leaped out of the car and hit the court rolling. There was a large crowd already there when we arrived. Lots of kids were competing in several different age groups. My wife found a good spot to set up our lawn chairs near the court. About thirty minutes went by before the competition began. The format was simple. Each skater got three one-minute runs that were scored by a panel of three judges.

Just about the time the first kid was going to make his run, I first noticed them. A group of about five punk-ass-looking goons all wearing Mohawk haircuts, all smoking cigarettes, and all cursing loudly behind the bleachers that had been set up for the spectators. I didn't give them too much thought. Several minutes had gone by, and four or five kids had made their first runs when I noticed a commotion near a holding area for skaters waiting their turn. I first heard someone cursing in a very vile manner. I looked over just in time to see one of the goons press a lit cigarette against the neck of one of the teenage kids. Assuming there was about to be a fistfight, I stood up from my chair. My wife held my arm and said, "Don't." The kid who had been burned was very upset, rightly so. However, at that very moment, the announcer called the kid's name. It was his time to skate. He turned and ran onto the court and started his run. So that separated the goon from the kid, and I sat back down.

I had hoped that was the end of it. Nope. The idiot then scaled the six-foot chain-link fence that circled the court. Once on the other side, he went after the kid. This brought the whole competition to a halt. The announcer began asking him to get off the court. He just responded by waving a double-handed middle finger. Now the parents in the crowd started yelling at him. He just responded to them by grabbing his crotch and yelling, "Suck this!"

That was it. Something had to be done, and I was the only officer anywhere round. I was off duty, out of uniform, and unarmed. As the fool was taunting the crowd, I walked onto the court and approached him from behind. I grabbed the collar of his jacket and began pulling him backward off the court. As I pulled him I told him very clearly, "I am a police officer, leave this park now." At the edge of the court I slung him out of the gate. I had used the title police instead of game warden purposefully, assuming this idiot had never been outside the city limits and would have no idea what a game warden was. I immediately pulled my ID out of my pants pocket and held it up for him and his buddies to see. I again repeated, "I am a police officer, leave this park now."

He charged me and slapped my wallet out of my hand. "I don't give a @#$% who you are!" This resulted in me grabbing his skinny neck with my right hand and walking him backwards all the way to the parking lot. In the parking lot, I took him to the ground. As I sat on top of him, I had a problem. His buddies now had me circled and were punching and kicking at me. I yelled to a man with a cell phone and said, "Sir, call the police." He responded, "I already have."

Now all I had to do was survive long enough for the troops to arrive. It seemed like a lifetime. As the band of thugs ran around in circles kicking and cursing me, my attention was

57

divided. At the same time, the guy on the ground was trying to spit blood at me from a busted lip. Each time I saw him pucker up to spit, I would try to cover his mouth with my hand. Then the unthinkable happened. He reached up and got my right ring finger in his mouth. He bit down so hard I actually saw my fingernail come off in his mouth. I stood up and tried to pull my hand away, but he wouldn't let go. I can honestly say I never felt that much pain before or since.

Without many options, I planted my left foot across his forehead. He let go. Have you ever taken a fish off a line and dropped it on the ground and watched it flop around? Exactly what this guy was doing. I actually thought for a second that I might have just killed him. It did accomplish one thing immediately. His friends scattered in all directions. I was standing up now and very pissed. All my concern for the idiot goon on the ground went away quickly when he regained consciousness and started cursing me again. About that time a Paris PD squad car pulled up and out got a patrol sergeant who I knew personally. I walked over, holding my bloody hand.

"Damn Benny, what happened to you?"

"He bit me."

"Who bit you?"

"Him!"

"You gotta be kidding me, not him again."

"What do you mean, 'not him again'?"

"He just got out of our jail last night."

"Well, he's going back. He is under arrest for assault on a peace officer."

More cops arrived and scooped up the guy, who I'm sure was suffering from a headache. They transported him to jail and held him, pending charges, while I rushed to the emergency room to get my finger sewed up.

A few weeks later the district attorney from Lamar County called me and said, "I need to tell you something, but you are not going to like it." He went on to explain that he gave the cannibal a plea deal in order to get a conviction. The guy got twelve months' probation for assaulting me. The DA figured correctly that the guy would never make it off probation before screwing up again. A few months later I got a second call from the DA, who advised, "He didn't make it... he is on his way to prison."

I carry a scar to this day that is a painful reminder of that day at the skate park.

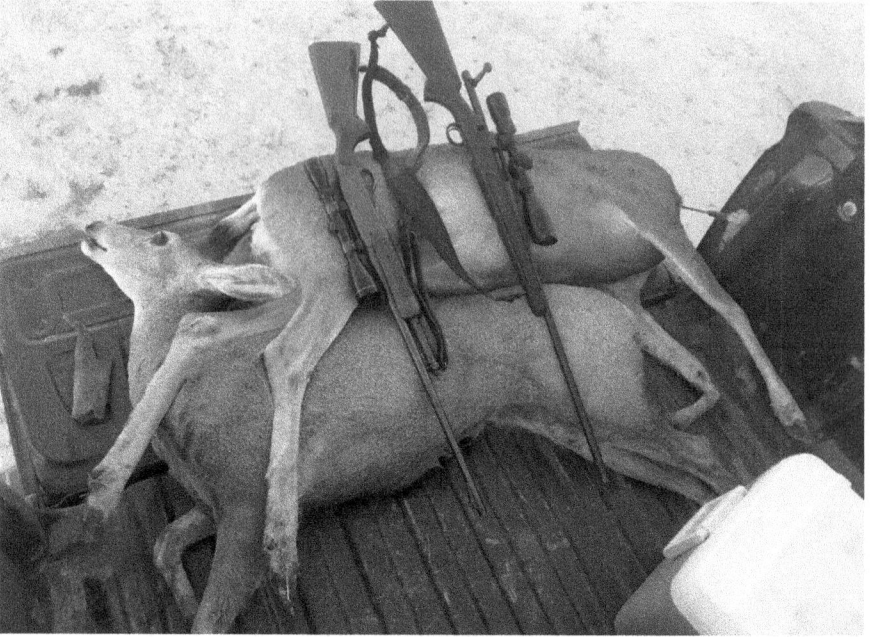

Mule deer does taken in closed season. (Dell City, Texas)

Horseback patrol on public hunting land. (Klondike, Texas)

Fish relocation at Big Creek Lake. (Cooper, Texas)

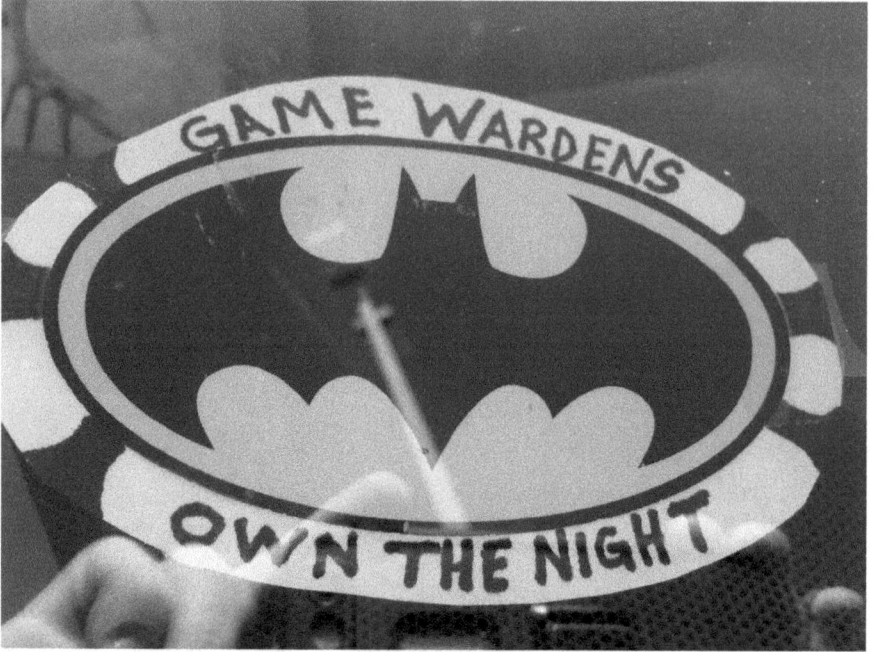

Tag that hung in patrol truck window as a warning to poachers.
(Bogata, Texas)

Nighttime poachers were on a roll until the long arm
of the law intercepted them. (Cooper, Texas)

Little owl named "Smash" that was given a second chance at life. (Rosalie, Texas)

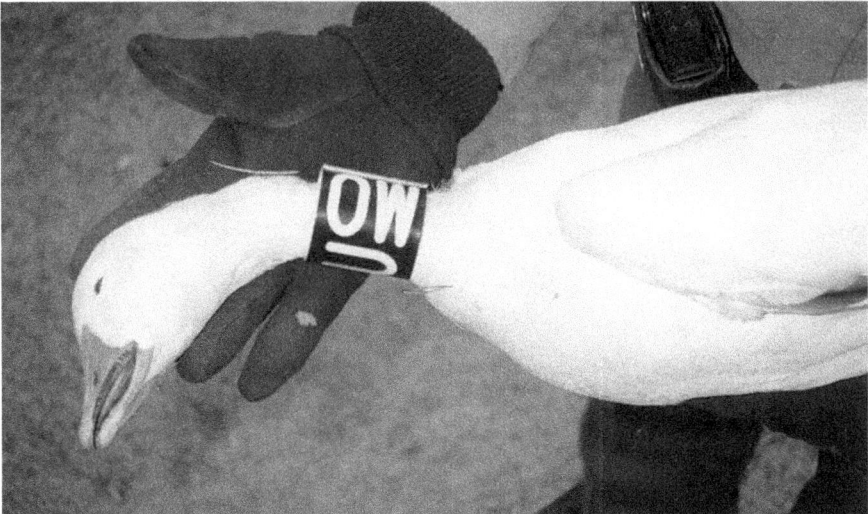

Collared and banded snow goose taken illegally with a high-powered rifle. (Dalhart, Texas)

A friendly coyote pays a visit. (Bogata, Texas)

Red River County wardens pose with "Surefire" after a long night's work. (Detroit, Texas)

This truckload of Mallard ducks was confiscated from hunters in Red River County. Charges of exceeding bag limit and baiting were filed. (Clarksville, Texas)

Warden Richards looks out over hundreds of boats
during Aquapalooza on Lake Travis. (Austin, Texas)

Being the daughter of a Texas Game Warden leads
to all kinds of wildlife adventures. (Rosalie, Texas)

Game wardens in Red River County get very busy during deer season.
(Detroit, Texas)

Wardens in deep East Texas with a bald eagle thought
to have been shot by an illegal hunter. (Jasper, Texas)

On horseback above
the Rio Grande River.
(Lajitas, Texas)

An orphan gets
its breakfast.
(Canton, Texas)

Standing guard at the end of the border wall. (Fort Hancock, Texas)

Cadet wall locker. 44th Texas Game Warden Academy class (Austin, Texas)

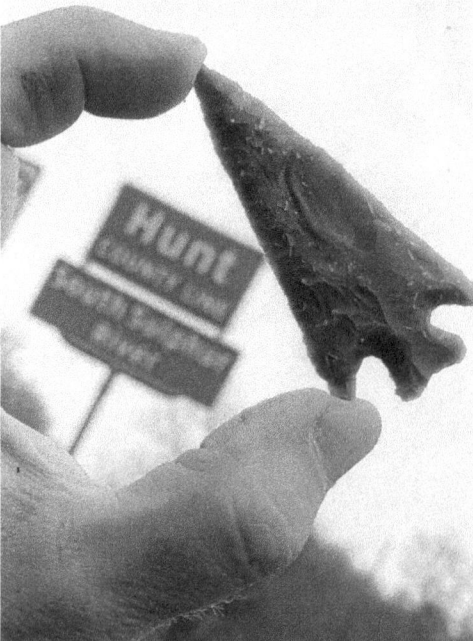

Arrowheads were a common find during foot patrols (Wolfe City, Texas)

Successful end to a bow hunting trip. (Horton, Texas)

A great duck hunt in West Texas. (Fort Hancock, Texas)

Rookie street cop in 1993.
(Richardson, Texas)

Officer Richards' patrol car after being struck by a DWI driver.
The wreck that almost ended it all. (Richardson, Texas)

A good buck hangs at the ranch in Christmas morning. (Horton, Texas)

A sixteen year old sophomore in high school. Destined to become a Texas Game Warden. (Wolfe City, Texas)

Last day on patrol after a 25 year career. (Campbell, Texas)

REPUTATION IS EVERYTHING

YOU JUST CAN'T DO IT. Asking one man to cover a whole county effectively is asking a lot. And counties in Texas tend to be larger than most. There is simply no way to be everywhere all at once. And what about those days off? Who covers your area then? If you were consumed with questions like these the way I was early in my career, you had some sleepless nights. A warden needs some extra help sometimes when none is available. However, I learned that over time he could give himself a bit of help if the warden had one thing... the right reputation.

Reputations are tricky things. They can break both ways. You can be known as a tireless worker or a lazy bastard. You could be thought of as an asshole or a good ole boy. You could have the reputation of being fair or unjust. In my opinion, a game warden's reputation is everything. A good reputation for being helpful can generate tips from standoffish landowners. A well-known reputation for not taking any crap might keep a drunk hillbilly from testing you out on a back road late at night. And so on and so on. I wanted to be known as a man who didn't sleep much, might show up at any place at any time, was fair in his dealings but fearless in enforcing the law. One thing for sure, you earn the reputation you get. Good or bad, you own it. I started building mine the first day I hit the field. I tried to be everywhere at once and rarely took an entire day off. I ended up working late into the night on many, many occasions.

One of those long nights found me on patrol in the north end of Delta County on a gravel road that came to a dead end on the banks of the North Sulphur River. The county often pulled gravel out of the bottom of the river and stockpiled it on the riverbank at this spot. Those gravel piles created a perfect hiding spot for my patrol truck. That night I was quietly sitting in my hiding spot, closely watching the county road for activity. Even though it was extremely cold, I had the windows down in order to hear any shots in the distance. All I could hear during the first hour was the sound of the water flowing down the river channel. It had rained a fair amount that week, and the river was up about a foot. Eleven o'clock came, and so did a vehicle. I watched carefully as a truck made its way slowly down the road all the way to my location. When the driver attempted a U-turn at the dead end, I realized I recognized the old farm truck. It belonged to a local rancher named Scotty Waller.

I had met Scotty a few times earlier and regarded him as a potential friend. I got out and walked around the gravel pile and flagged him down. He was surprised to see me, and I had to explain that my truck was hidden and I was working. For his part, Scotty was out checking on his herd of cattle. He leased the pastures on both sides of the road for grazing. Scotty, being a night owl like me, often checked his cattle late at night. We stood outside his truck, just shooting the bull and gossiping about local politics. All at once, pointing over my left shoulder, Scotty said, "Hey, looky there. You got company." Across the river channel the bright beam of a spotlight could be seen working along a tree line a quarter mile away. We continued to observe the light until *BOOM!* A shot rang out and the light disappeared. Now it was game on. I wasn't sure what was just shot, but I intended to find out. I could see that there were two four-wheelers across the river. After picking up their kill, they began to move along the north side of the river channel, headed east. While we stood in the darkness taking all this in, Scotty asked, "What are you going to do?"

"I'm going to catch them."

I had to get going if that was going to happen. I told Scotty I intended to cross the river on foot. I also asked him to hang around long enough to make sure I made it across the river.

"Do you want me to wait here?"

"I don't know when I'll be back, so you don't have to wait if you need to go."

"I can't believe you're crossing that river. Do you know how cold that water is going to be?"

"Yeah, I know. Hey, if my truck is still here in the morning, something went bad wrong. Can you come check?"

"Sure I will. You better be careful."

"I'll flash my light at you to let you know I made it across."

"OK."

I walked to the river's edge and thought to myself, *Would any other game warden I know do this?*

The answer was no, and that absolutely meant I was going to do it. I made my way down the bank and entered the water. The ice-cold water took my breath away. I hesitated long enough to gain my composure, then began wading. The water was crotch deep. If the water had been flowing any faster, it would have taken me off my feet. At the opposite bank, I used hands and knees to get to the top. I was a muddy mess. Once out of the river, I turned and gave Scotty the signal.

I had some catching up to do. The suspects were a good distance ahead, holding a steady pace along the river's edge. I began a slow jog, trying to close the gap. A quarter mile later I was no closer but still had them in sight. At a fence line they turned north. I cut across the plowed field at an angle and gained a little ground. Even though it was freezing cold, I was now out of breath and sweating profusely. After topping a hill, they disappeared. Dammit! Please don't let this happen. If I lost them, I would have done all this ridiculous and dangerous shit for nothing. Then I caught a break. As I reached the top of the hill, there they sat. The driver of one four-wheeler held a light as the other driver attempted to open a gate. I was able to slow down but reached them just in time. As I reached them, I shouted, "GAME WARDEN!" They both almost fainted.

"Put your guns on the ground, now!" They did it without hesitation. A dead doe rested across the back rack of one of the four-wheelers. Completely exhausted, I leaned over and rested my hands on my knees as I tried to catch my breath.

One of the guys asked, "Are you OK?"

"Hell no, I'm not OK. I just swam a river and chased you a half mile. Would you be OK?"

I barked out a few other things on my mind as the two men stood quietly. After things calmed down and I was semi-sure that I wasn't about to die of a heart attack, the conversation got more cordial. They were caught red-handed, and they knew it. It was just a matter of the details now. I told them to leave the doe lying on the ground on my side of the gate. I didn't have a truck handy at the moment, and I wasn't going to let them transport my evidence another inch. I allowed them to load their four-wheelers onto a trailer that was hitched to their truck a short distance away. My last instructions were for them to meet me at the Lake Creek Post Office in one hour, or else.

As they drove away, I made my way back to the river with the knowledge I had to cross again. It was every bit as cold and deep the second time. I was never so glad to crawl up into that cab and turn on the heater. I picked up the receiver of my old Cellular One bag phone and dialed up Scotty. I let him know I was back at the truck and filled him in on the details. He said, "I still can't believe you did that."

"Yeah, well, if I had to do it again, I might think about it longer."

I met the night hunters at the post office as scheduled. Two citations were issued for hunting deer at night. I then returned to the gate and collected the dead doe. The cases were made, investigation completed, and my work for the night finished. I went home.

Did I have to go to the extremes I did? No, not really. Was there an easier way? Yeah, maybe. However, I got a lot out of that situation and the way it all unfolded. I knew if I caught the guys the way I did, it would shock the hell out of them. I also knew they would spread the word far and wide about that wild-ass game warden on the opposite side of the North Sulphur River. I knew Scotty would also tell all the locals at the coffee shop about that crazy game warden they had now.

After a few more episodes like that one, I began to get that reputation. After a few more years, I definitely had that reputation. It was then that I could get a more restful sleep a lot more often. That reputation was guarding my county when I could not. Believe it.

JUST ANOTHER
DAY AT THE LAKE

I NEVER REALLY did enjoy boat work for a lot of reasons. Checking other boats was a hassle, especially in choppy water on windy days. The two boats were always moving around while you were trying to conduct your business. You had to be constantly vigilant not to let your patrol boat slam into the side of the other boat and cause damage to a fiberglass hull. Another thing about boat work was it was mostly done in the summer months under a scorching sun. Getting sunburned was just part of it. I will say one thing about boat patrol. It provided some interesting sights. Add some alcohol, and boat patrol provided some very, very interesting sights.

One July, I was sent to Austin, Texas, to patrol Lake Travis during a huge event called Aquapalooza. Lake Travis was known for being a little weird and wild even on the slowest weekends of the summer. This particular event brought in thousands of boats of every kind, from yachts to rowboats. My partner and I were easing through the mass of boats anchored near a floating stage where a country music star was giving a concert. We pulled alongside a large houseboat that had an upper deck. On that deck about a dozen girls were dancing and singing along with the music. They were all in various stages of undress. One girl in particular was wearing a pair of white, furry, knee-high boots. That's all she was wearing. About the time we noticed her, she noticed us. She walked to the railing and began shaking her body parts at us. Then, I guess in order to get some kind of response from me, she shouted, "Hey, what do you think?" I simply replied, "I like your boots."

"Oh, really? Here, you can have them!"

She took off each boot and hurled them at us. She then ran inside the cabin. On any other lake in Texas she would have been arrested on the spot. However, given all that was going on all around us, it seemed par for the course. Going after her would have been more trouble than it was worth. And it actually was kinda funny if you think about it.

Another time on Lake Lavon in Collin County, several game warden teams were patrolling at night on a boating-while-intoxicated task force. In the distance, near the center of the lake, I could see the blue flashing light of a game warden boat. With not much activity of our own, we went to assist the other wardens. It turned out to be Game Warden Rick Lane and his partner. They had a houseboat full of girls stopped and were doing a water safety inspection. We pulled alongside, tied up, and boarded the boat also.

The atmosphere on the boat was festive. The girls on the boat were taking part in a floating bachelorette party on the rented houseboat. The girls, who had obviously been drinking a bit, were laughing and taking pictures with all the game wardens when another houseboat passed close by. A man on the passing boat yelled, "Hey, do y'all got a joint you could sell? Let's party!" All the game wardens just looked at each other. This was a clue.

"Sorry girls, we gotta go." All four wardens boarded the patrol boats and went to pay the captain of the other boat a visit. After stopping and boarding the boat, we all were speechless at what we discovered. Yes, the operator of the boat was drunk and there were drugs present, but what was strange was the huge assortment of adult sex toys that filled the cabin. Some of them made me blush. I never knew such things existed. That captain spent the night in jail. Yes, looking back over those years that I spent patrolling in a boat reminds me that you never could predict what you were going to find on the next boat you contacted.

Sean Reneau and I were working on Cooper Lake, headed straight for a couple that were fishing in a secluded cove near the dam. I was driving the boat and Sean was up front making the contacts. As I pulled parallel alongside the boat, Sean greeted the man and advised him we needed to do a water safety check. The man got up and started retrieving his life jackets and other gear as the woman remained seated at the front of their boat. I was relaxed and not paying much attention when Sean suddenly started asking the man about the smell of burning marijuana. My ears perked up and I started looking around their boat. Between the driver's seat and the steering console, I saw a piece of tinfoil lying flat on the floor. On top of the tinfoil were a Bic lighter, a glass pipe, and some unknown substance in a bag. I rose to my feet and started making my way to the front of our boat. Sean looked back at me and I said, "10-95." This was code for "He is going to jail."

I guess the guy could see the writing on the wall. He bolted to the back of his boat, scooped up the foil and all its contents, and jumped overboard. I leaped over into his boat as I was shucking my gun belt. I then went right overboard with him. I grabbed him underneath the water. My auto vest inflated, which shot us to the surface. Sean was waiting to pull the idiot back into the boat. I was able to locate a prescription pill bottle containing marijuana floating nearby. In addition, the guy had several partially dissolved hydrocodone pills in his shorts pockets. After handcuffing the suspect, Sean began laughing, looked straight at me, and said, "Dumbass... why did you just do that?" Sean was right, it wasn't really necessary to dive in after the guy. But hell, how are you ever going to get the right reputation if you don't do something a little crazy every now and then?

Last, but not least, there was that sunny morning on Lake Tawakoni. I had Warden Chris Fried along for the ride that day. We were patrolling near the two-mile bridge when I saw a bass boat cutting across the lake. I fell in behind it and started closing the distance. The female driver looked back and saw us approaching. Suddenly, she got up and switched seats with the guy in the boat. As we got very close and prepared to stop the boat, I witnessed the girl put something in her bikini top. Chris Fried conducted a water safety check. Neither of us mentioned what I had seen until the check was completed. However, once Chris was finished, I asked the girl, "Young lady, what do you have hidden in your top?"

"Nothing."

"I saw you put it in there.... Whatever it is, we can handle it with a citation, or you can go to jail. It's your choice."

I guess she didn't like the thought of going to jail. She reached in and removed a small amount of marijuana wrapped in plastic. Chris boarded their boat to collect the evidence. At this point he spotted a glass pipe in a cupholder.

"What's this? Do y'all have any more dope on this boat?"

Both just shrugged their shoulders, looked down, and offered a very weak "No."

"That's not good enough. I'm going to look."

Chris turned and opened the top to a live well at the front of the boat. Inside were six large freezer bags stuffed with marijuana. In a rod box next to the driver's seat, Chris located three bundles of cash wrapped with rubber bands, each bundle the size of a man's fist. Over six thousand dollars in all. Now, here is a twist, I thought. I hadn't figured on a dope dealer transporting his goods back and forth on a public lake. I could go on forever with similar stories such as these. Each one just another day at the lake.

JAYWALKER

WHAT FIRST GOT MY ATTENTION was the dogs running across the pasture. Looking out the passenger window I could see three of them. Slowing down for the sharp curve ahead, I then noticed the guy standing on the right side of the highway, clearly holding a rifle. As I rounded the curve, the tall weeds in the ditch blocked my view temporarily. When I came out of the curve northbound, I saw the same guy now standing on the left side of the highway, but not holding a rifle. Hmmmm... that's strange. As I approached him, I took stock of the guy. Short and dumpy, with a potbelly, kind of dirty and unshaven. I rolled down my window and pulled up to the man. His yellow teeth glistened in the afternoon sun as he began to lie.

"What's going on?" I asked.

"Oh, nothing. My dogs jumped out of my truck and I'm just trying to round them up."

"Where is your truck?"

"It's over there."

"Why is it over there?"

"I didn't want to block the road."

Over there turned out to be half a mile away, parked in a field between two rows of five-foot bales of hay. Obviously an attempt to hide the truck. A total of five dogs, all wearing tracking collars, were now running around, circling my truck.

I wondered if this guy thought I was a fool. He obviously didn't know who he was talking to. I went into investigation mode my way. I didn't always do things like they taught them in the academy. My methods could be questioned, but the final results could not.

"Well, partner, all your dogs are here now. Let's get them loaded up and you back on your way." I got out and lowered the tailgate and slung one of the dogs up into the back. The man was looking a little nervous but followed my lead and loaded the other four.

"Hop on in." We got inside the patrol truck and I slowly crossed the ditch and drove toward the man's truck. As I drove, we made polite conversation about everything except what was really going on. After arriving at his truck, the man was all smiles and thank-yous. I did a quick U-turn in the field. Just before driving away, I rolled down my window and posed one last question.

"Hey man, tell me something straight up. Have you been hunting?"

"No, sir!"

"You wouldn't lie to the ole game warden, would you?"

"No, sir!"

"OK then, have a good day."

I pulled away very slowly. I figured he would either come to his senses, or I would go retrieve a good rifle from the ditch and consider it abandoned property. As I drove away, I continued slowly across the field, checking the rearview mirror. When I had travelled about two hundred yards, it started. He began waving his arms and jogging toward me. I stopped and waited. Sweating and breathing heavily, he came to my driver's window and confessed.

"Sir, I need to tell you something."

As sarcastically as I possibly could, I replied, "Now what on earth would you need to tell me?"

"Well, sir, I guess I was hunting."

"You mean you lied to me? Say it ain't so."

He ducked his head and said, "Yeah, that's my gun up there."

"Go get your truck and all your dogs and meet me at the highway."

I drove back to the bar ditch and located a Ruger, bolt-action, stainless-steel rifle. While I waited, I placed a phone call to the landowner, who revealed the man was hunting hogs with dogs without permission. He got his gun back, along with two crisp citations. I wish I had known that day what I learned over the course of the next few years. That man was one of the most notorious poachers that ever operated in Northeast Texas and Southeastern Oklahoma. That was the first meeting of several that would follow.

EXPERIENCE MONEY CAN'T BUY

THE BEST GAME WARDENS the world over didn't learn in any academy the things that made them successful. Sure, the academy offered tactics and techniques, a brushup on rules and regulations, an instruction on required paperwork. However, the skills and knowledge that a really effective warden needs are learned over time, beginning shortly after birth. Call it life experience.

My peers who I worked with over the years that I had the greatest amount of respect for and confidence in all showed up day one at the academy already well trained in some areas. They were experts in firearms and how to use them, having used everything from a single-shot break-over .410 up to an AR-15. A lever-action .30-30 or a bolt-action .30-06 and everything in between. Skilled at operating boats of all kinds because of years of previous experience on lakes and rivers taught to them by their fathers and grandfathers. Masters at wildlife identification because of a life spent in the woods hunting and on the water fishing. Some people will know what I'm talking about when I say there is a big difference between the way a wood duck flies as compared to a canvasback. Other people have no clue what a canvasback is.

This is not to say there are not some great wardens who eventually picked up the trade after leaving the academy, regardless of previous outdoor experience. It's just that the people I have just described have a clear and definite advantage going into the field of conservation law enforcement. Every kid exposed to hunting and fishing learns something from each trip afield. A sight, a sound, or a smell. It's all stored inside their brains. Over time, an encyclopedia of knowledge begins to form between their ears that can be retrieved when needed.

I started building that knowledge at a very early age by following my father and uncles through dark woods to deer stands and duck blinds. I accompanied them on harrowing boat rides in every kind of weather. By the age of ten I was fascinated by hunting. If my eyes were open, I was thinking about hunting. If my eyes were closed, I was dreaming about hunting. Many years later I realized all those hundreds of hours I spent in the pursuit of fish and wild game was experience money can't buy. You just have to live it, and live it I did.

One such experience happened on a bitterly cold winter day in January. A strong arctic front had rolled through and covered everything with a half inch of ice. The roads were almost impassable, so school was called off. My father and mother could not make the twenty-five mile drive to their workplace. So our whole family was at home. The temperature outside was in the low twenties. Near lunchtime there was an urgent knocking at the front door. I answered the door to find two friends of mine standing on the doorstep. They lived next door. They excitedly told me a lot of ducks had just landed on a long pond at the base of a hill just south of our house. At ten years old I was fanatical about hunting, and both of my friends knew I would be interested in their scouting report. About that time my father came to the door to find out what all the discussion was about.

"Dad, Gary says a bunch of ducks landed on the pond."

"Oh yeah? How many were there?"

With a big, toothy grin Gary just replied, "A lot... a whole lot."

My father walked away, but I could tell something was up. He had a plan. I thanked my two friends for the info and closed the door. My dad began to put on warm clothes and told me to do the same. I knew this meant we were going out into the cold. Things got even more interesting to me when he came out of the bedroom with two guns. I bundled up and put on my rubber boots. We walked to the old '64 Chevy pickup and got in. I was a little worried about the ice-covered road even though my father was not. Leaving the driveway slipping and sliding, we drove the quarter-mile distance that got us near the pond. Hastily, my father tried to explain the plan he had hatched, which included walking around to the back side of the pool bank. There we would use the low berm to sneak up on the unsuspecting ducks. Sounded good to me, but I realized one thing quickly. Saying it is one thing. Getting it done is another thing.

We crossed the barbed wire fence, which caused the four-inch icicles to break and fall to the ground. We slowly made our way around to the back side of the pond. Each step sounded like walking on potato chips. *Crunch... crunch... crunch.* As we approached, it became obvious that the plan wasn't going to work. We needed to cover another hundred yards to have any hope of being in gun range. We sounded like a herd of buffalo crushing through the ice-covered grass. With fifty yards to go, the first wave of black-headed ducks lifted off. My father exploded into a full sprint and said, "Let's go get 'em!"

He was the first one over the berm. The firing began immediately. When I came over, I was in amazement. There must have been over one hundred ducks running across the surface of the water in all directions, attempting to get airborne. I watched as my father emptied ten rounds out of his .22-caliber rifle. He never ruffled a single feather. He looked over at me and yelled, "Shoot!" I wanted to, but at which one?

I lifted the barrel of the twenty-gauge single-shot and fired off my only round at the center of the flock as they exited the south end of the pond. I clearly missed. This is when we discovered we had made a serious tactical error. Just feet in front of us, ducks started popping up from beneath the surface. These were diving ducks. Out of ammo, all we could do was watch as each one said goodbye and flew away. My father spit out more four-letter cuss words than I had ever heard in my life in one standing. Our pride damaged and confidence broken, we staggered back to the truck.

I learned a lot of lessons that day. I learned a .22-caliber rifle is very ineffective at taking flying water fowl, in addition to being illegal. Sometimes you learn what not to do by watching others do what they shouldn't do. I also learned if you are very limited on ammo you had better pick out one bird and make your shot count. When school in Wolfe City resumed, I did some research and identified those curious black-headed ducks as lesser scaup, also known as bluebills.

Although we were completely unsuccessful, that short, frozen duck hunt is still a good memory. Like I said before, experience money can't buy.

ATTITUDE ADJUSTMENT

HAVE YOU EVER HEARD someone say, "A game warden can go into your house and check your freezer if he wants to"? Or how about, "A game warden is the most powerful law enforcement officer there is. He has more authority than anyone." I wish I had a dollar bill for every time I heard these things. When I was much younger and uninformed, I assumed both were true. The fact is neither is true.

Let's start with the first statement. No one, no law enforcement officer anywhere, nobody can simply waltz into your home and check your freezer, or anything else, without a properly obtained and executed warrant. Period, end of story. It is true that in Texas game wardens have some special inspection authority not granted to other officers. A Texas Game Warden can inspect and, in some instances, search a barn, outbuildings, vehicle, tent, cooler, or game bag without a warrant if he has reason to believe wildlife resources are being hidden or concealed in violation of wildlife laws. I guess over the years some folks stretched that to include your freezer in your home. But it just ain't so. One other important distinction between game wardens in Texas and other law enforcement officers is the right to enter private property to enforce wildlife laws.

I was once told of a situation where a group of police officers wanted to get inside a house to search for drugs. For whatever reason, they couldn't get a warrant. The owner of this particular house was known to keep a pet fox squirrel she had raised.

One officer got the bright idea to use the local game warden's wildlife inspection authority as a pretext to get inside the house. The new and very inexperienced warden went along with the plan. The warden showed up at the house and demanded to inspect the squirrel, thought to be in a cage inside. He took one of the local police officers with him. Once inside the house the police officer began looking for drugs as the warden inspected the animal. Drug paraphernalia was found in plain sight, and then more officers came in, based on that. Drugs were discovered, and the resident was arrested. Shame on the police officers for using the warden the way they did. Shame on the game warden for being so foolish. He endangered the authority of every warden in the state when he allowed himself to be used in that way.

Now, about the statement that a game warden is the most powerful law enforcement officer there is. Here again, there is not much basis for that claim. There were times during my career when I wondered if I had any power at all. When I was stationed in the Texas Panhandle one of the local judges I worked with would routinely dismiss the cases I would file. It's hard to claim you are the most powerful law enforcement officer around when you can't even get a conviction on a class-C misdemeanor charge. That type of situation wasn't reserved for the top of Texas. In later years, back on the other side of the state, the district attorney in my county would dismiss serious felony cases I filed. When I asked for an explanation, I was told, "It is in the interest of justice." Well, if that's justice... I ain't interested. So much for being the most powerful law enforcement officer there is.

I hope no one will get me wrong. I was very proud to be a Texas Game Warden and would not have traded my position for any other law enforcement job. In truth, a warden's real power comes from his ability to use the vast amount of discretion he has to enforce the law. Most game wardens work with minimal supervision. They can decide on a course of action without a lot of consultation and hand-wringing from others. Game wardens who use their discretion wisely and consistently are usually admired and respected in the community. That is where the real power and authority comes from. All this being said, there are those folks new to Texas that have no clue about game wardens' unique role in law enforcement across the Lone Star State.

Once upon a time in Hunt County, I was patrolling on a Saturday morning. I was near an area that contained a lot of hunting camps. As I rolled past one camp near the long county road that wound through the timber, I noticed a large four-wheel-drive truck parked next to a camper trailer. Nearby, a campfire from the night before was still smoldering. Of most interest to me was the pile of squirrels and two shotguns lying on a picnic table. I stopped at the gate and got out to do a hunting license check and game inspection. The gate was locked, so I climbed over and walked twenty yards to the trailer. I took a look at the squirrels, then walked over to the front door and knocked. The door swung open with a young boy standing in the doorway. I asked, "Hey pardner, is your dad around?"

Suddenly a man appeared. He had a scowl on his face when he asked, "Who are you?" I identified myself as a Texas Game Warden and explained that since there was a two-man limit of squirrels outside, I needed to check his hunting license. He pushed his son aside and said, "You have no right to be on my property!" I assured him that, as a game warden, I had full authority to be standing right where I was standing. I again asked to see his hunting license. He blurted out, "You didn't see me hunting, why do I need a hunting license?"

I replied, "Well, have you been hunting?"

"It's none of your business!"

"You are wrong, sir.... It's my only business."

"I'm not showing you anything, and I want you off my property."

"You will show me your hunting license or your day is going to be a bad one."

At this point he threw me a curveball by telling me he was a police officer. I asked him to show me his badge. Sure enough, he pulled out a legit badge. I was shocked to see another officer acting this way and asked him why.

"I was a police officer for fifteen years in Pennsylvania and two years in Texas, and I know the rules."

I replied, "Well, I'm not sure you do. I don't know how they do things in Pennsylvania, but I have the right to enter this property and check your hunting license. I'd like to see it right now."

The man went into a rage and stated he wanted my name and badge number because he fully intended to have my job. Listening to his rant gave me an idea.

I asked, "Hey mister, what is your name and badge number?"

"Why do you need that?"

"Because this name-and-badge-number thing you want to do gives me a good idea. Let's call your department and see what they have to say."

His tone immediately changed. I didn't back down an inch. After getting his name, badge number, and lieutenant's name,

I made a phone call to his department and got his supervisor on the phone. I asked the lieutenant if he had an officer named Dudley Peditt working second shift. He confirmed that yes, he indeed did have an officer by that name working second shift. I went on to explain the situation that I had and asked the supervisor for his assistance in getting some cooperation from his officer. He asked if I would hand the phone to Officer Peditt. I handed the phone off and stepped a few yards away. From a short distance away, I could hear the conversation clearly.

"Have you lost your damned mind?"

"No, sir."

"That man is a Texas Game Warden! You show him anything he wants to see. Do you understand?"

"Yessir."

"When you get here tomorrow you come to my office. We're going to talk about this."

"Yessir."

"Please hand the phone back to the warden."

The lieutenant apologized for his officer's unprofessionalism and said to call him back if I encountered any more problems. I explained there were no hard feelings and I would wrap things up quickly and be on my way. Wow, what a difference one phone call can make. The officer quietly pulled out his hunting license and presented it to me. Looking over the license, I noticed a deer tag was missing, but the harvest log was not completed on the back of the license as required by law. Texas deer hunters will know what I'm talking about. I issued a written warning for that infraction. Anyone else would have gotten a full-blown citation, but I wanted to extend an olive branch. The man signed the warning, we shook hands, I climbed back over the gate and got into my truck and drove away.

In the end, I think the officer simply hadn't been Texanized quite long enough. He just didn't know enough about Texas Game Wardens. He probably wasn't a bad guy. He just needed a little attitude adjustment.

TRACKS ACROSS THE PRAIRIE

THE ONLY THING that concerned me about the call was the hour of night. The only thing that made the call unique was that it was one of the county commissioners that was missing. My family had just gotten home from a ballgame and we were about to eat a late supper when the call came in. The dispatcher from the Red River County Sheriff's Office called me on the phone to advise that officers were requesting my assistance on County Road 1200. She went on to explain a county commissioner had not returned to his home from work that day, and his truck and trailer had been located but not him. I got into uniform and headed out to meet the other officers. County Road 1200 was a gravel road that I was very familiar with. It stretched across the Bogata Prairie from east to west. The area was basically large fields of open cropland with some scattered trees along fence lines.

It had been dark for about two hours when I arrived on scene. Several officers were gathered near a pickup truck with a sixteen-foot trailer attached. The truck and trailer were parked at the edge of a plowed field. The trailer was empty, but there were metal ramps attached at the back that were lowered to the ground. There was information that a four-wheeler was normally carried on the trailer. The man that was missing not only served as a commissioner for Red River County, but he was also a professional surveyor. On this

98

particular day he had been completing a survey on a large block of land out on the prairie. He had been working alone. When he did not return home before dark and did not return her phone calls, his wife got worried and called the sheriff's department, which sent everything into motion. Officers responded to the area where he had told coworkers and acquaintances that he would be located for most of the day. After finding his truck unattended and four-wheeler gone, officers fanned out, searching the maze of other roads nearby, without any luck. Obviously something was wrong, and we needed to find him.

As our small group of officers discussed scenarios, a deputy's voice came across the radio. He had found some survey equipment set up at the edge of another field approximately a half mile to the south. Perhaps this was a lead that would provide some answers. At that same moment I had noticed a single set of tire tracks that cut across the plowed field, headed south. As officers loaded up into their squad cars to drive around to the newly discovered survey equipment, I asked Bogata police officer Dustin San Jule to stay with me. We patiently watched as the other officers made their way around to the other field. Once their headlights in the distance indicated they had made it to the other location, the tire tracks I had found became possibly more important. The tracks headed across the prairie in a straight line that would take a person riding a four-wheeler from our location over to the other officers.

Dustin and I left the gravel road and began following the tracks across the plowed field. Walking thirty yards apart, we used our flashlights to look for any signs of the missing commissioner or his four-wheeler. Just over halfway across the field, we came to a drainage ditch that was unexpectedly deep and eight feet wide. The ditch was completely obstructed from view by the thick, tall weeds growing along the sides. I knew that prairie better than anyone on earth, having hunted there for so many years. However, that deep ditch took me completely by surprise. I never knew it was there.

I waded through the thick weeds and prepared to cross to the other side. Suddenly, I heard Dustin shouting, "I found him! He is over here!" I pulled my cell phone off my belt and called the dispatcher as I ran to Dustin. When I crashed through the weeds, I found Dustin standing beside a four-wheeler that was turned upside down on the opposite side of the ditch. The commissioner was pinned underneath it. Unfamiliar with the area, he had driven his four-wheeler into the ditch that was hidden by the tall weeds. Within minutes, officers came from everywhere. We unfortunately were too late. He had been crushed by the weight of the four-wheeler upon impact. He had passed on, and Red River County lost a very good public servant that afternoon on the prairie.

RIVER OF NO RETURN

I SAT QUIETLY in the brush and cane at the top of the riverbank. Twenty feet below, the murky waters of the Rio Grande River flowed slowly by. Me and three other wardens were on a stakeout. All week we had witnessed hundreds of people crossing the river illegally from Mexico into the state of Texas. They were from countries all over the world. This spot where we lay in wait was one of the most active places for crossings in the sector we were assigned to.

We were interested in one particular raft. Numerous times over a five-day period we observed the same guy paddle across the river with a load of five or six border crossers. These guys that navigated rafts and transported these people were known as "coyotes." Our team had come close to nabbing him several times, but each time he managed to unload his human cargo and escape while giving us the big middle finger. This day was going to be different.

I tried to remain motionless, but the mosquitos buzzing around my face made that impossible. At the top of the bank on the Mexican side, a man searched our side with a pair of binoculars. Without detecting us, he disappeared into the brush. Just seconds later, the coyote appeared with a rubber raft. He dragged it down to the water's edge. He was followed by four women, a small child, and one other man, all walking single file to the raft. After everyone was loaded, the coyote pushed away from shore and began to furiously paddle. In about two minutes, he was within twenty feet of our side. He would never bring the raft any closer before ordering his passengers out. So it was now or never. All game wardens exploded from our hiding places and descended on the raft. As soon as the coyote saw us, he knew he was in trouble and panicked. Looking for a way out, he turned and snatched the small child out of the arms of its mother. He turned and flung the child over the front of the raft into the river. One warden dove in and rescued the child. Another warden and I jumped in the water and jerked the coyote's skinny ass out of the raft. The last warden used a makeshift spear made from cane to puncture the rubber raft several times. All the others made it safely onto shore. On the opposite bank a Mexican scout used a cell phone to report back to thugs in Reynosa.

We dragged the coyote to the top of the riverbank. Holding him down in the red clay mud, I handcuffed him behind his back and said, "Welcome to Texas... you are under arrest." A game warden captain and border patrol agents were summoned to the scene. After some consultation and a phone call, the captain told me to transport the coyote to the county jail in Edinburg and charge him with human trafficking. It was a task I was more than happy to complete. Scenes like that were not common along the Rio during border assignments. It seemed like as time went on we were told to take a more hands-off approach, which baffled me. Are we not serious about stopping all this? I guess it was to be expected since politicians were involved.

Make no mistake, that river was dangerous. Drownings were another unfortunate event down there. One morning Warden Kurt Kelly and I had just unloaded our patrol boat into the river for patrol. After parking the truck and trailer, I walked back down to Kurt, who was staring at something floating against a metal grate at the end of an irrigation canal.

"What is that?"

"I don't know, but it don't look good."

We walked over to the water's edge and confirmed that it was not good. It was a decomposing body. Clothing was the only thing holding it together. There was no telling how long the poor soul had been in the river.

Another time Warden Chris Fried and I were on the river, tied up to cane along the edge. We got a phone call about a woman screaming downriver on the Mexican side. We fired up the engine and made the very short trip around a bend, where we saw a Mexican woman down on her knees on a sandbar. She was still screaming and pointing toward the center of the Rio Grande. On the Texas side, a border patrol agent was standing at the edge of the water, also pointing to the center of the river. We correctly assumed someone had just gone down. Using the body drag we had in our boat, we got lucky. I snagged clothing on the very first pitch and pulled the victim off the bottom up to the surface. It turned out to be the hysterical woman's husband. The border patrol agent yelled across and directed her to use the international bridge to come across to Texas and collect her loved one. Things were so damned callous on that border.

I lost track of all the drownings down south during my fifteen or more border assignments. There is one, however, I will never forget. Assignments back then were organized pretty much the same. One day shift and one night shift consisting of a captain on land, two wardens on land in a truck, two river boats, and six river wardens. On this tour of duty, Warden Jimmy Woolley and I were the land unit. Our job was to transport food, fuel, and other equipment to the river boats, as needed. We also were the communications connection between game wardens on boats and all other agencies working the border. Other than that, we spent our time patrolling and occasionally assisting border patrol with foot chases.

Midafternoon one day, we were sitting stationary on a levee that ran parallel with the river. Suddenly, the captain's voice came across the radio with some urgency.

"Hey, Jimmy, y'all try to get ahold of the boat units and tell them to come to Anzalduas Park. We may have a drowning."

"10-4, Captain."

I started the truck and headed to the park two miles away as Jimmy summoned the troops. Anzalduas Park on the Texas side had been shut down to the public and was being used exclusively for law enforcement activities. All agencies parked vehicles and launched boats there. On the Mexican side, it was a long, extensive park that usually attracted hundreds of people on the weekends.

We met the captain inside the park at the river's edge. On the opposite side of the river there was chaos. Everyone in the park was now lining the riverbank. Several grown men were wading out into waist-deep water, searching. On a sandbar a poor woman was screaming and pulling at her hair as she rolled around on the ground. You didn't have to be too intelligent to figure out what was going on. Shortly, many of the Mexicans on the other side began yelling across the river pleading for our help. The captain told Jimmy and me he needed to go to the top of a hill to get service in order to make a phone call. As he left, he instructed us to call him when our boat units showed up.

It was painful to watch the heartfelt agony in the other side of the river. We were told it was a child that was missing.

Within minutes, one of our patrol boats could be seen approaching from the north. Assuming that our wardens would be assisting in a recovery, I ran to a truck and retrieved a body drag. Once the river boat arrived, Jimmy and I filled them in on the limited information we had. I handed them the body drag. The captain returned and, after a brief discussion, our patrol boat and crew were sent to help search for the child. At this point, several trucks loaded with Mexican police showed up at the park across from us. Verbal communication was established between Mexican police and our wardens on the boat. The wardens lowered the drag into the water and went to work. They made one pass without success. On the next pass they found the little boy. The child had been under the warm water for the better part of an hour. Nothing more could be done.

Conversations between the Mexican police at the park and the wardens on the boat led to a phone call to our captain seeking instructions. The captain gave the green light to take the child to the shore in Mexico. Good for him. The boat crew navigated to a spot down the shore and away from the crowds. A Mexican police officer waded out to the boat and took possession of the little lifeless body. The boat and crew returned to the Texas side. The terrible ordeal was over for Texas Game Wardens. It had all been a sight too often familiar.

Weeks later, it came to my attention there had been a lot of second-guessing and armchair quarterbacking over the captain's decision to allow our wardens to help recover the drowning victim and return him to his family over on the Mexican side of the river. What was he supposed to do? Ignore the cries of grieving people looking for a lost child? The captain didn't let politics get in the way of doing the right thing. The human thing. I was proud of him for that.

Over the course of about five years, I learned to hate the Rio Grande River near McAllen, Texas. It was ugly, polluted, and dangerous. No one in any government was serious about stopping what was going on down there, so in my opinion it was a colossal waste of resources and game wardens' time. My feelings will not be hurt if I never see that place again. That stretch of river brings back nothing for me but bad memories, and for many border crossers it became a river of no return.

JUST GOT OFF AN AIRPLANE

IN OCTOBER 2014 my son was a cadet at the United States Military Academy at West Point in New York. During his time there he was a member of the Sprint football team. Regardless of the distance, I tried to make it to as many of his games as possible, even though it required a plane ride, rental car, and hotel stay.

After watching the Army cadets pound Cornell University 49–7 one afternoon, I boarded a jet airplane in New York City and headed back to Texas. I turned my cell phone off just before we left the ground. During the flight I leaned the seat back and dozed off. Not long after I woke, the pilot was guiding us in for a landing at DFW airport. I collected my bag and navigated through the crowds out the front door to the parking area, where my wife was waiting. Before getting in the truck, I remembered to turn my phone back on. It was then I saw that I had missed a call from one of my better landowners. I immediately dialed him back. When he answered the phone, I asked, "Hey, Larry, what's up? I see I missed a call from you."

"Benny, where are you?"

"I just got off an airplane in Dallas. Why?"

"I've got a problem. They just shot a deer on my place about an hour ago."

"Who did?"

"I don't know. They were using a spotlight. They ran when they saw me coming."

Larry went on to explain that a white truck came by his house, shining a spotlight. He watched it through a kitchen window as it stopped on the county road, and two shots were fired across his pasture near a spot where deer usually bedded down. He went to confront the night hunters. He saw three guys run out of the ditch, get back in the truck, and flee. He was unable to get a license plate number. I told him I was on my way but asked him to turn off all the lights at his house and keep watching in the meantime. I thought there was a chance they might come back. I told Kristi to let me drive home. The seventy-mile trip home took less time than normal, as I might have been speeding just a bit. When I was about five minutes from the end of my driveway, Larry called me again.

"Hey Benny, they are back."

"Are you sure it's them?"

"Yeah, but they are in a black car this time. They are out in my pasture walking around right now."

"Well, hey, don't go down there unless they try to leave. I'll be there in ten minutes."

"OK, I'll watch them."

After pulling up in my driveway, I bailed out. I knew I didn't have much time before the poachers would be gone. I ran through my house collecting what I needed: my badge, my pistol, a flashlight, and a ball cap with the Texas Game Warden patch on front. There was no time to put on a uniform. I jumped in my patrol truck and hurried over to Larry's place, not too far away. As I got close to his house, I blacked out my headlights and slowed to a crawl. When I passed in front of his home, the front porchlights blinked on and off several times. That was Larry's way of telling me he knew I had made it in time.

About two hundred yards farther, I encountered a small black car sitting in the middle of the road. Looking south across the pasture, I could see the beams of flashlights bouncing up and down headed my way. The culprits had heard me drive by and were looking to make a run for it. It was much too late for that.

I pulled up within twenty feet of the car and lit it up with every light I had to offer. One of the suspects had stayed behind at the steering wheel. I caught him completely off guard. I was standing at his driver's window when he turned on his headlights. They were caught. I got the young driver out as two other teenagers climbed over a gate. I gathered the three stooges in the middle of the road as Larry pulled up on his ATV. I lined them up and prepared to start the interrogation. But first, I had to make one thing perfectly clear since I wasn't in uniform. Holding my flashlight toward my ball cap, I picked the dumbest-looking one of the trio and said, "Hey pardner, I want you to read aloud what the patch on my hat says."

He began to read, "Texas Game Warden... Law Enforcement Division."

I interrupted him, "Are there any of you who don't know who I am or why I'm here?"

They all acknowledged they were fully aware I was a Texas Game Warden. At this point, after a short conversation, I followed them back out into the pasture, where they pointed out a small amount of blood from a deer they had shot earlier. We searched but never recovered the deer. After giving up on finding it, we again assembled in the roadway. Acting on a hunch, I then demanded to know where the white truck was and where the rifle was that had been used to shoot the deer. They first denied being in a white truck. But with Larry applying contradictory pressure, they then spun a tale about a mysterious friend. This mysterious friend supposedly owned the white truck and the missing rifle. Curiously, none of the three could remember this friend's name or his phone number.

I had had enough of lies. I pulled out my handcuffs and told them if they didn't tell me immediately where the truck and rifle were located, they were all going to jail. This loosened their lips and improved their memories. They told me to follow them to the high school parking lot in Lone Oak, Texas, ten miles away. At the high school, the white truck was parked near the football field. Inside, leaning against the seat, was a .30-06 rifle. After removing the weapon, I shined my flashlight into the back of the truck. My hunch was correct. Fresh blood and deer hair could easily be seen coating the bed. I then gave the boys a short speech.

"Well, guys, it looks like we have another deer y'all need to explain. So... start explaining, and remember what I said about jail earlier? That wasn't a threat. That was a promise."

I was then told to follow them down a dirt road where a wooden bridge crossed a creek just north of town. At the bottom of the creek lay the lifeless body of a white-tail doe. The entire deer had been carelessly wasted and dumped. These guys weren't hunters. I wouldn't even flatter them by calling them illegal hunters. They were punks out on a killing spree. They needed their asses whipped with a leather belt.

I instructed them to drive back to town and meet me at the all-night convenience store there. Then I used my cellphone to begin calling parents. After everybody had arrived at the store parking lot, I explained everything to the parents. I showed them the cell phone pictures I had taken and explained the possible penalties. They stopped short of begging me not to put their sons in jail. After consulting with Larry, who had originally called me, I opted not to put anyone behind bars.

However, I did use most of the citations out of a new ticket book.

In summary, my day started in New York and ended in Lone Oak, Texas, and this little night of drive-by shootings got very expensive.

WHAT GAME WARDEN?

NIGHT WORK for a Texas Game Warden in the Texas Panhandle is a lonely proposition. I spent a lot of time all alone staring up at the stars while stationed in Dalhart. Good night cases were hard to come by for a couple of reasons. For one, the small human population. The more people gathered together, the greater the odds for someone to do something stupid and illegal. Dalham and Hartley Counties were three thousand square miles of prairie and hills with very few people. Second, one man trying to cover that much ground was a guessing game. Sometimes you just had to try and think like a poacher and hope to get lucky.

Late in December 2002 I was pulling an all-nighter. I had patrolled the area near Texline on the border with New Mexico without any success. Cutting through that vast country, keeping an eye on the horizon, looking for the glow of a spotlight, I finally found myself crossing over Rita Blanca Creek, west of town. This area had one big canyon running through it and was known for big muleys and giant white-tail bucks. I decided to find a hiding spot and wait a while.

Backing up over a cattle guard and into a gate on a bluff provided me with the cover I needed and a clear sight of the highway below for three miles in each direction. Listening to the local weather report from Amarillo, I wasn't surprised to

112

hear the forecasted low for that night was twelve degrees. I sat silently for two hours while a light snow fell outside my truck. Not one single vehicle passed by. I wasn't at all surprised by this. Highway 998 was the back way from Channing over to Dalhart. It was nothing but ranchland and very remote. Any vehicle moving this late at night would have been met with my suspicion. My exact reason for sitting here.

It was 2:05 a.m. when I spotted it. The glow of headlights approaching from the east. The vehicle topped the ridge and headed down into the canyon. My eyes were trained on the vehicle, looking for any indications that it might be a night hunter. It cleared the bridge at the bottom of the canyon and headed up and out and never broke stride. I was a little disappointed when I leaned back against the seat. Then the vehicle did something completely unexpected. It came to an abrupt stop in the highway right below me. Now I was excited again.

Grabbing the binoculars off the dash, I went to work. I could see it was a small, red four-door car. Not your customary poaching rig. It was occupied by a single white male. He never got out, never shined a light or fired a weapon. He just sat inside with the interior light on.

I have never been accused of having any patience, and that night was no exception. I was tired. I was cold. I was curious. With my headlights off, I slowly made my way down off my perch and down to the highway. He was totally unaware of my presence when I pulled up twenty feet behind him. This was it... let's find out what he is doing.

I turned on my headlights and red and blues simultaneously. The driver ahead never hesitated. He put the vehicle in gear and floored it. The chase was on, and I knew it was going to be a dangerous one. A thin layer of snow blanketed the road surface. Nonetheless, this guy was running, and running hard. I notified

113

the dispatcher in Dalhart of the situation and my location as I pursued at eighty-five miles per hour.

About four miles into the chase, it almost came to a crashing halt. I could see into the fleeing vehicle well enough to determine the driver was trying to get something from the passenger side. He swerved over onto the right side of the road. He then overcorrected just before hitting the ditch. This caused him to go into a spin. The vehicle did two perfect 360-degree spins, and wouldn't you know it... ended up stopped in the middle of the highway facing north.

When he regained his composure, the suspect was off and running again. It wasn't long before a handgun flew out of the driver's window. I responded by throwing a plastic cup out my window as a marker. A mile later, a white object was thrown out and then another. I tossed my ball cap out the window to mark the spot. Speeds now were nearing one hundred miles per hour when I called dispatch and asked for the intersection with Highway 54 to be blocked. I wasted my breath. Local deputies, troopers, and police were already there, waiting with spike strips if needed.

In the end it was a fairly undramatic close to a chase. With the highway ahead lit up like the Fourth of July, the guy reduced his speed and rolled to a stop. When he exited his vehicle with hands raised, I approached him, pistol drawn. He asked me, "Why are you chasing me?"

I replied, "Because you are running from me! Now turn around and put your hands behind your back."

Once he was secured and on his way to jail, I informed the other officers about the items that were thrown from the vehicle. I told them I would meet them at the jail later. I was able to relocate my markers and recover a stolen pistol and two bags of powdered cocaine.

Back at the jail, the arrestee's mouth got loosened up, and he explained he had been taking the back way to Dalhart to avoid police between there and Amarillo. He went on to explain that he had stopped to sample a bit of his product when I showed up.

What game warden? Oh, that game warden. It happens so often—cautious and concerned when it comes to being caught by police but no consideration at all for the local game warden. Time to reconsider.

DEER CROSSING

IN THE LIFE of a game warden, a deer being hit by a vehicle is a most aggravating call, right behind injured bird calls. They are all too frequent, sometimes very messy, and in the end there is a lifeless carcass that you have to do something with. As my career as a game warden progressed, the way I handled these calls evolved. Early on I thought if a collision involved a deer it was my jurisdiction, and I needed to be there each time to investigate the matter. How naïve I was. What complicated the matter was the fact that it is written into Texas law that it is illegal to possess any part of a wild deer that has been struck and killed by a vehicle. I usually just ended up being a janitor of sorts. A trooper or other officer completed the accident report and/or called a wrecker if either was required. My job was just to remove the dead animal from the scene and attempt to donate it so it wasn't wasted.

Donating a dead deer with its guts hanging out at midnight in August and ninety-five-degree heat is not going to happen. Dispatchers used to ring my phone frequently to notify me of the latest smushed deer, usually at night. Sometimes more than once in a night. If I did respond, I'd burn a quarter tank of fuel that could have been used more effectively. In later years I learned to try and handle the whole matter over the phone. If I got a phone call from someone who just struck a deer, I would ask two questions: "Do you need an ambulance?" and "Do you want the deer?"

Many times the person did, indeed, want the deer. This was great for me. I didn't have to make a trip, nor did I have to track down someone to give the deer to. If it was another officer calling to advise me of a deer-versus-vehicle crash, I would offer the deer to the officer or anyone he could find to take it. I was surprised over the years at how many officers took me up on the offer and hid the deer on the side of the road until their shift ended and they could come back to get it. In either case I would collect a phone number in case I needed to follow up in any way. Over the span of my career, I guess I received three hundred or more calls about deer getting mowed down on the highway. That's just a guess. Two of these calls stand out.

Early one morning I responded to a deer crash on Highway 24 north of Commerce, Texas. There were reports of a serious injury. There were several other law enforcement agencies on scene when I pulled up, including a state trooper. An ambulance left en route to the hospital with the driver. Upon exiting my patrol truck, I observed a small four-door car sitting sideways on the shoulder of the highway. What really got my interest was the dead deer lying on the back of the car. In order to get the details, I walked over to the trooper, who was completing a report. He advised the driver had suffered a serious head wound. I assumed he had struck his head on the steering wheel or something due to the impact. I then asked the trooper, "Who put the deer on the back of the car?"

"What do you mean?"

"Why did someone lay the deer on the car like that?"

Laughing now, the trooper said, "You don't understand. The deer went through the car and ended up there. No one has touched it because we were waiting on you."

I stood in disbelief. Walking over to get a close look, it was obvious what had happened. Blood and glass from the front windshield covered the front seat. What was left of the back glass was scattered on the pavement behind the car. The deer was lying lifeless, half inside the car and half on the trunk lid. I collected the buck and left the scene.

On another morning, I was sleeping in, having worked a very long night. Around eight o'clock my phone rang beside the bed.

"Hello?"

"Are you the game warden?"

"Yes sir, how can I help you?"

"Well, I'm out here on Highway 2577 with a deer my wife ran over."

"Is the animal dead?"

"Oh, yes sir, he is plenty dead."

At this point, slightly aggravated from being awakened, I went into my standard protocol.

"Is your wife OK?"

"Yeah, she went on to work and called me about it. I came down here to look. It's just around the corner from our house."

"Is the deer a buck or a doe?"

"It has big antlers."

This caused my eyes to open just a little bit from being closed and unconcerned.

"How many points does it have?"

"Well, let's see... hmmm... hmmm... thirteen, fourteen, fifteen.... It has fifteen, I think."

This caused me to sit straight up in bed, eyes wide open.

"Sir, can you stay with that deer until I can get there?"

"Yes sir, I'll wait."

"Give me fifteen minutes."

I was putting my uniform on as I was getting in the truck. Driving slightly faster than the speed limit, I got there quickly. I could see the guy standing in the ditch as I approached. As I got closer, I could see one side of a massive set of antlers sticking up above the grass. The man was correct. The unfortunate buck had fifteen distinct points with wide, heavy beams. For anyone with knowledge of the Boone and Crockett scoring system, the buck scored 195. It was the largest free-roaming white-tail buck I had ever personally dealt with. It was a shame that the monarch died the way he did. I collected the buck and left the scene.

My family was not immune from striking deer crossing the road. My wife, Kristi, and I bought a brand-new, shiny, red Jeep CJ-7 as a wedding gift to each other. Fresh off our honeymoon trip, we were driving along one afternoon with her behind the wheel. Suddenly I spotted a doe standing beside the shoulder of the highway.

"Watch that deer."

"What deer?"

"Watch that deer!"

"What deer?"

BAM!!

"That deer!"

We had to replace a front bumper, front fender, and rear-view mirror.

My daughter, Kaitlin, called me in tears one morning. A deer jumped out in front of her and almost totaled her little Nissan Juke. Five thousand body shop dollars later she was back on the road.

Nowadays when I see a deer on the side of the highway, all I see is a check for my deductible amount.

THEY ARE ALL BAD

IN THE SPRING of 1992 I was pursuing my goal of becoming a Texas Game Warden. I had finally finished the needed four-year degree required to apply. The hiring process for the forty-third academy class was about to begin, but I wasn't just sitting around twiddling my thumbs. I wanted to learn all I could in order to better my chances of being selected. I found help in the form of a game warden named Dale Waters. I called him out of the blue one day and asked if I could ride along with him on patrol. To his credit, Dale never hesitated and invited me to jump in his truck the very next day. I found Dale to be likable and very knowledgeable. It didn't take long before we had established a friendship.

One Sunday morning on Mother's Day, Dale called me up and asked me if I was up for some boat patrol on Lake Tawakoni. "Of course!" I said. I met him at the sheriff's office in Greenville and we headed south. We had just backed up to the boat barn to hook up his johnboat when a call came in over the radio. A dispatcher advised of a 911 call about a possible drowning at the lake. The location of the emergency was at a spot on the lake known locally as the slabs. The area contained a lot of underwater obstructions, including large, concrete sections of a roadway that had collapsed and submerged after the lake was flooded in the 1950s. Dale knew the area well, and we rushed to the scene. When we arrived along the shoreline, we observed an old man standing in knee-deep water looking out across the lake. Just ahead of him a group of four or five people were gathered at the water's edge. Pointing out across the white-capped water, the old man shouted to us, "The boys are there!"

Puzzled, Dale asked, "How many are there?"

"There are three. They are out there."

"How long have they been down?"

"I'd say about twenty minutes."

Dale turned to me and said, "This is bad, let's go!"

We rushed to get the boat into the water, but common sense was telling us it was too late. This wasn't going to be a rescue. This was going to be a recovery. The lake was angry that day. A stiff twenty-mile-per-hour wind blew from the south. It was difficult to use the body drag as the rolling waves pushed our small boat around in circles. Eyewitnesses attempted to direct us from the shoreline seventy-five yards away. We were trying to locate the bodies of three teenage boys, two brothers and their cousin, who had been wade fishing in the heavy surf before going down. The uneven bottom, combined with the underwater obstacles, complicated things. Eventually we located two of the boys in about six feet of water and brought them to the shore to their grieving family. Dale's partner finally arrived, and together the three of us recovered the third victim. To this day, that was the saddest drowning I ever worked. On the way home that afternoon, Dale warned me, "When you go to work for us, you're going to see a lot of these. They are all different, but they are all bad." No truer words have ever been spoken.

Fast-forward to 1997. I had almost, but not quite, completed my rookie year as a Texas Game Warden. It was late summer, and I was working a game warden booth at the Hunt County Fair, one county west of my county of assignment. Around 8:30 p.m. I was approached by a sheriff's deputy who advised my captain was trying to get hold of me. These were the days before pagers and cell phones. I went to my truck and called the captain on my old Cellular One bag phone.

"Hey, Captain, what's up?"

"Benny, you have a drowning on Cooper Lake. I need you to go hook up with the two wardens I have already sent and y'all three work it."

I left immediately and drove back to Delta County to hook up to my johnboat parked at my house. Radio calls I placed to the other two wardens went unanswered. I drove to the John's Creek boat ramp, where a firetruck and ambulance had already arrived, along with the local justice of the peace. Two almost victims had been plucked from the water by passing fishermen and were standing in the parking lot, wrapped in blankets. I interviewed the two men, who told me the following story.

Three friends had launched their boat just after dark to do some night fishing. They anchored in the center of boat lane number one and began to fish. A short time later they realized their boat was filling up with water. They had forgotten to put the drain plug in the boat. Instead of starting the boat and making a run for shore, they began using cups to try and bail the water out. All three of them were leaning over the same side, bailing water, which caused the boat to capsize. They all were thrown overboard without life jackets. Two men came to the surface and began to tread water. They never saw their partner again.

I also took a statement from the fishermen who rescued the pair. They gave me valuable information by telling me they

THEY ARE ALL BAD

had towed the capsized boat to the dead timber at the side of the boat lane and tied the nose of it to a tree to keep it from sinking. I was told by survivors and witnesses that I would find the drowned man's body near the center of the boat lane. I launched my boat in the darkness and headed east down the boat lane. Five hundred yards down the lane I encountered the other two wardens using a body drag to probe around the boat that was now fully submerged except for the nose, which was secured to a tree trunk with a rope. The other wardens had launched from the opposite side of the lake, two miles away, and went to work, having not spoken to any witnesses. I attempted to relay the information I had been given. They completely ignored me. I tried again, telling them the boat had overturned in the center of the lane. One spoke up.

"We wouldn't even be here if you'd stay in your county."

I quietly thought to myself, *What did that little half-ass dipshit just say to me?*

I suddenly grew weary of people I considered underlings getting in my way. I decided to do it all myself. I positioned my boat in the center of the boat lane and tossed out my anchor. Using a flashlight and pocketknife, I cut off five large hooks and an old rusty window weight from a trot line I had lying in the bottom of my boat. With electrical tape from my small toolbox, I secured the hooks to the weight. I tied the weight to the bow line and slowly lowered it into the water. It took a couple of tosses, but I finally felt something tugging on the line as I pulled it to the surface. A bare foot emerged from the murky water below me.

"Hey guys, I've got a dead body over here. Could I get a hand, please?"

The two other wardens paddled over and helped me remove the victim and place him across the front of my boat. I delivered the deceased to the ramp, where the local judge pronounced him dead. Warden Waters was exactly right. All drownings are different, but they are all bad.

ALL ABOUT THE BENJAMINS

WHEN CHRIS FRIED called me and asked about patrolling the rest of the evening, I said, "Sure, come on, but we have something we need to do." I had been working on a missing person's case involving a teenage girl from Greenville, Texas. Those types of cases were not my normal duties, but the girl's father had called me personally and asked me to get involved. I guess he wasn't satisfied with the help he was getting from the local authorities. When Chis arrived, I was following up on a tip that she had been seen walking near a house in a shady neighborhood on the west side of town. We ended up taking his patrol truck. After making numerous laps around the neighborhood and talking to some locals, we couldn't locate the girl.

"Let's make another run by the high school."

"Okey dokey."

Chris stopped at an intersection and prepared to make a left-hand turn onto a one-way street. An oncoming pickup truck turned in front of us going the wrong way on that same street. Chris said, "Look at this idiot!" We turned right and began following the wrong-way driver. When Chris hit his red and blue lights, the guy driving the truck slammed on the brakes and bailed out, leaving his truck rolling down the street with the driver's door open. The whole thing happened so fast it caught us off guard. The wrong-way driver ran out into a vacant lot, stopped, and turned around to look at us. Honestly, we were both laughing, and neither of us was even thinking about getting out. We watched as the runaway truck rolled to a stop against a curb.

Chris rolled down his window and, still laughing under his breath, said, "Hey, come over here." The man just shook his head side to side. A little more sternly, Chris again tried to get the guy to come to us by motioning to him and saying, "Get your ass over here!" Again he just stood and shook his head side to side. At this point, Chris and I began to get out. That did it… the guy was off and running. OK, this kind of disrespect could not be tolerated.

I shouted to Chris, "Stay with the truck!" I began the foot chase with full confidence that this short, dumpy, wannabe track star was no match for me. He made it about one hundred yards before he ran out of gas and I was sitting on top of him as he was facedown on the sidewalk. I was giving him a little bit of an ass chewing as I searched him for weapons. There were no weapons to be found, but there was a surprise. This fellow had sixteen thousand dollars, all in hundred-dollar bills, in his shorts pockets. Hmmm… wonder what type of business he was in?

There was no chance for a question-and-answer session. The guy didn't speak a lick of English. Chris drove up, and again he was laughing. Then off to jail we went. Greenville police assisted in towing the abandoned truck. At the jail our guy was charged with traffic violations and evading arrest. His cash was confiscated and a report sent to the local district attorney's office. That was that, and back out on patrol we went.

A couple of days later I was contacted by an attorney who was representing the guy we arrested. I knew the attorney well and was on good terms with him. He wanted to know how he could get his client's money back. I advised him that if the district attorney's office issued a letter releasing the money, I would get it back to him promptly.

The wheels of justice were spinning fast that day. He called me back in less than an hour and said he had a letter in hand from the DA. Later that same day I counted out sixteen thousand onto the attorney's desk. The guy was never prosecuted, to my knowledge, of the evading charge.

Oh well, all in a day's work.

Retired?

THERE ARE NUMEROUS DOCUMENTS tucked away in file cabinets that indicate that a little over a couple years ago I retired as a field game warden with the Texas Parks and Wildlife Department. There was even a popular TV show that tracked my entire last day on the job and sent video proof of my retirement to living rooms around the world. I gave back my state truck and keys. I no longer put on that uniform. My cell phone number was given to another warden that took my place, and so on, and so on. Yeah, it appeared that after twenty-five years I was retired.

The morning after it was official, I still got out of bed. I didn't look any different. I didn't feel any different. So-called retirement was not an earth-shattering event for me. Within a few weeks, I had become accustomed to my new routine. I had also received my new badge and commission as a Special Game Warden. That title basically allowed me to still carry the blue badge and enforce the state game and fish laws under limited special circumstances and in the absence of an active field game warden.

It was about that same time I started getting that same question over and over. "Do you miss it?" Honestly... I have not missed all the bullshit paperwork and new computer crap that always comes along with government over-management.

But... yes, on cold, clear nights in the fall, the thought of crawling back in that patrol truck once again is appealing. I guess warden work will always be in my blood.

Since riding off into the sunset I have had a couple of opportunities to flex my old game warden muscles. Late one afternoon I was returning home from a deer hunt when I witnessed a very large tanker truck sitting beside the road near a bridge. As I passed by, I noticed a big green hose connected to the bottom of the truck and running down into the bottom of the ditch.

"Hmmm... that doesn't look right." I turned around and contacted the driver of the truck to find out what substance was being dumped into the ditch and flowing into the creek. His explanation of the situation, in broken English, was completely unsatisfactory. I made a quick call to the local field game warden, who proceeded to get an arrest warrant and arrest the driver based on the information I had given him. Strike one in the win column for the environment.

A couple of months later I was enjoying a warm campfire when I noticed suspicious activity across the highway on some property owned by a large utility company. I watched as a man cut the lock off a gate and entered the property on foot. Again, I made a call to the local warden. He showed up with night-vision equipment, and together we went into the woods and arrested the trespasser. The violator turned out to be a subject I had previously arrested numerous times during my career. Back to jail he went.

Occurrences like these two make me totally question the word *retirement*. Actually, for me personally, the term is incorrect. It indicates an ending. I don't use that word anymore. I still have a passion for enforcing the law. I still have that deep pride of being a game warden. It's true I'm not on anyone's payroll any longer, and my role has changed drastically. However, I will be a game warden until the day I die. When that day comes, my headstone will have the title *Texas Game Warden* carved in stone above my name. It's not what I did. It's what I was.

THE END

OTHER BOOKS BY
BENNY RICHARDS

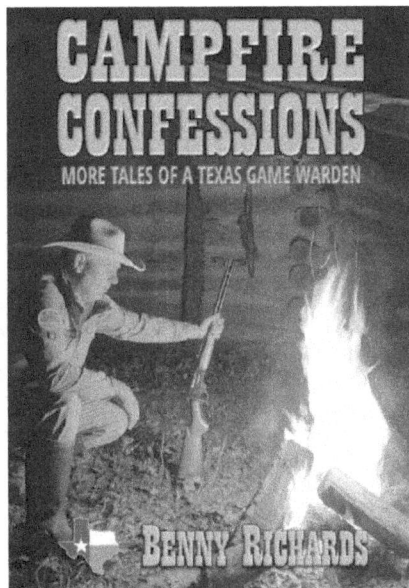

www.ingramcontent.com/pod-product-compliance
Lightning Source LLC
Chambersburg PA
CBHW060236030426
42335CB00014B/1487